To my Eva,
who loves the land of Israel,
the people of Israel,
and most importantly,
the Messiah of Israel.

Israel has always been a flashpoint of controversy situated amid the Arab nations of the Middle East. Issues such as its right to the land, its connection (if any) to the Israel of the Old Testament, the application of the promises given by God—these matters are also debated in the West and often earnest Christians disagree. No matter where you stand on these issues, you owe it to yourself to read this book, written by someone who has studied the Bible and history focusing on these controversies. I have personally been present when Michael Rydelnik has discussed these issues with professors who disagree with him and I left more convinced than ever that his interpretation of Scripture and history is correct.

ERWIN W. LUTZER
Pastor Emeritus, The Moody Church, Chicago

I'm so grateful for Dr. Michael Rydelnik for publishing this urgently needed book that clarifies the role of Israel and the Jewish people in God's plan. I have spoken to many wonderful Christians who are confused and in need of biblical guidance to help them know how to think and speak about Israel. These believers pray for Israel, support Jewish missions, share the gospel with Jewish people, but when they hear about Israel being accused of cruelty, they do not know how to answer the charges. Dr. Rydelnik's brief volume will help you respond to those who are wondering whether Israel should matter to them.

MITCH GLASER
President, Chosen People Ministries

The verbal attacks being launched against Israel today are as deadly as the physical attack launched by Hamas in October 2023. The rapid rise in hatred and antisemitism against both Jewish people and the Jewish state is shocking. If you've been disturbed by what you've seen and read but feel unprepared with answers, then this is the book you need to read. Dr. Michael Rydelnik has distilled the essence of all the false arguments being promoted and offers a clear, compelling, and rational response. Here are the answers you need to counteract the lies and half-truths currently masquerading as "facts" in this age of deadly disinformation.

CHARLIE DYER
Professor-at-Large of Bible and host of *The Land and the Book* radio program

In a time where antisemitism is rising and bad theology is being espoused from far too many pulpits, Christians, now more than ever, need to get the biblical truth on the Jewish people, the nation of Israel, and prophecy, fulfilled and yet to be fulfilled. There is no better teacher on all things Israel than Dr. Michael Rydelnik. This book needs to be read by every Christian to learn how to counter both media propaganda and mounting bigotry against the Jewish people. This resource couldn't have come at a better time.

JANET PARSHALL
Host/Executive Producer, *In the Market with Janet Parshall*

With Israel in the headlines daily, Dr. Michael Rydelnik provides the clarity and biblical insight we desperately need. In a world where emotion and opinion often cloud the issues, his theologically grounded words cut through the confusion and remind us of God's ongoing plan and purposes for the Jewish people. This is an important and timely book. I highly recommend it.

MIKE FABAREZ
Compass Bible Church, Aliso Viejo, CA

In these days of deception and delusion, Dr. Michael Rydelnik provides an indispensable resource to correct the false narratives of replacement theology and antisemitism, and he exposes the lies that have infected all levels of society. He expertly reveals God's prophetic plan and role of Israel within the scope of biblical mandates and provides clear guidance of how the church should view Israel. This is a must-read for those wanting to behold Israel from God's perspective.

AMIR TSARFATI
Author and speaker, President, Behold Israel

Michael Rydelnik never fails to deliver, regardless of the topic he's teaching. There's so much to glean and learn from *How Should Christians Think About Israel?* that it's worth all the time you can devote to it. Michael even clarifies the knotty issue of replacement theology, all with an accessible voice and tone that put the cookies on the lower shelf for us laypeople. This is a much-needed piece for times like these.

JERRY B. JENKINS
Writer of the Left Behind series and *The Chosen* novels; former chairman of the board of trustees, Moody Bible Institute

A Quick Guide to God's Covenants, Biblical Prophecy, and the Jewish People

HOW SHOULD CHRISTIANS THINK ABOUT ISRAEL?

DR. MICHAEL RYDELNIK

MOODY PUBLISHERS
CHICAGO

Emphasis in Scripture has been added.

Edited by Pamela Joy Pugh
Interior design: Puckett Smartt
Cover design: Darren Welch

978-0-8024-3983-3

Originally delivered by fleets of horse-drawn wagons, the affordable paperbacks from D. L. Moody's publishing house resourced the church and served everyday people. Now, after more than 125 years of publishing and ministry, Moody Publishers' mission remains the same—even if our delivery systems have changed a bit. For more information on other books (and resources) created from a biblical perspective, go to www.moodypublishers.com or write to:

Moody Publishers
820 N. LaSalle Boulevard
Chicago, IL 60610

3 5 7 9 10 8 6 4

Printed in the United States of America

Contents

A MERE QUIRK OF HISTORY?

"The modern State of Israel is merely a quirk of history, no more—no less!"

So declared a Christian college professor. He and I had been invited, as teachers from different schools, to hold a joint forum about Israel during one of the persistent conflicts the terrorist group Hamas had provoked with Israel. This professor maintained that the rebirth of the State of Israel in 1948 was a mere fluke, a secular oddity, and utterly irrelevant to divine providence, biblical prophecy, or the biblical people of Israel. In his view, the church is the true Israel; the land grant God gave Abraham, Isaac, Jacob, and their descendants belongs to the church, which will not receive the land of Israel but rather "inherit the whole earth." According to him, the Jewish people are no longer distinct in the plan of God, and they have no biblical right or even a relationship to their historic homeland.

Sadly, every time Israel is forced to defend itself from nations or terrorist groups that seek its destruction, there are those in the Christian community that share this professor's view. These mistaken ideas arise from a lack of understanding of several key concepts. First, people are often confused about what constitutes Israel, who the Jewish people are in the Bible, and how these people are connected to contemporary Jewish people and the modern State of Israel. They wonder if the Abrahamic covenant, found way back in Genesis (12:1–3; 15:1–21; 17:1–22; 22:15–18) has anything to do with current conflicts in the Middle East.

A second area of confusion concerns the Jewish people as a chosen people and raises several questions. What covenants and promises did God give this nation in the past? How is He working them out at present in our world? Are Jewish people redeemed by virtue of their birth, or must they, as everyone else, trust in the Messiah Jesus? And what does biblical prophecy reveal about God's plans for Israel in the future?

Yet a third area of misunderstanding is related to the relationship of the church and Israel. Has the church replaced Israel as the true chosen people of God? Or does God have distinct plans and programs for Israel as well as for the church?

Finally, people are puzzled about whether believers in Jesus should even care for the Jewish people. They think that Israel is just one of many nations. Since Jewish people for the most part do not believe in Jesus, why should we even be concerned for this people?

The purpose of this book is to clear up all this confusion and misunderstanding. In chapter 1, I will explain who the Jewish people are in the Bible and how they relate to the Jewish people and the State of Israel today. In chapter 2, I will address God's choice of Israel, the covenants He gave Israel, and how these affect the past, present, and future of the Jewish people. Chapter 3 will deal with the issue of the differences between Israel and the church, showing them as distinct entities. In the fourth chapter, I will offer several biblical reasons Christians today should still care about Israel and the Jewish people. Finally, to pull all this together, I will address why any of this is practically important to Jesus followers today.

Some of you may know that I host *Open Line with Dr. Michael Rydelnik*, a weekly Bible Q&A program. Although the program is designed to address questions about the Bible, God, and the spiritual life, I am amazed at how many listeners call with questions about the Jewish people and the State of Israel. So why do they call? I suppose it is because I am a Messianic Jewish follower of Jesus and have been a professor of Jewish Studies for more than thirty years, so they must presume I can answer their questions.

But the cause of listeners asking all these questions about the Jewish state and the Jewish people is the media's magnitude of misunderstanding regarding Israel and the bewildering information reported about the Jewish people. And it is not only the mainstream media. Preachers, politicians, and podcasters all feed the disinformation pipeline. People who love the Lord Jesus just want to have their questions about the Jewish people answered. That is what this book proposes to do. So, let's get started.

Chapter One

ISRAEL: THEN AND NOW

A United States senator was on a talk show explaining his support for Israel: "As a Christian, growing up in Sunday school, I was taught from the Bible that those who bless Israel will be blessed, and those who curse Israel will be cursed. I want to be on the blessing side of things," apparently referring to Genesis 12:3.

Cynically, the host replied, "Those who bless the government of Israel?"

When the senator clarified he meant the nation of Israel, not necessarily its current government, the host pressed further, feigning confusion, and demanded, "I'm confused . . . I'm a Christian, so I want to know what you're talking about."

Actually, this host was not confused at all. He was mocking the idea that there was any connection between the biblical promises made to ancient, biblical Israel and the modern Jewish State of Israel. In his mind, and in the minds of many Christians, there is no connection whatsoever between the two.

This Christian confusion is rooted in the lack of understanding of some key identifiers of Jewish people. They often see but fail to comprehend terms such as *Hebrew*, *Israel*, and *Jews*, as they are used in the Bible and in the twenty-first century. This leads to an even more serious bewilderment about the relationship of biblical Israel to modern Israel. Moreover, people are puzzled about how ancient scriptural promises to the Jewish people should be applied today. Who are these Jewish people and how should Christians relate to them now?

Let's define these key terms and then address some of the questions raised about them. That is what this chapter will do, beginning with a brief section on definitions, followed by an examination of the issues related to biblical and modern Israel.

TERMS AND DEFINITIONS

Bible readers will recognize a variety of terms used of the people to whom God chose to reveal Himself and then called to proclaim Him to the nations. All these words can be baffling. So a good place to start is with some definitions (these will be short and simple with fuller explanations in the endnotes).

Hebrew

The first word that needs to be understood is *Hebrew*, an ancient term applied to the patriarch Abraham. It's likely from the root of a word meaning "to cross over" because of Abraham crossing over from the Euphrates River.[1] Although *Hebrew* fell out of use as a term for the Israelite people by King David's time, it was applied to the language spoken by the Israelite people, even as it is still known today.[2]

Israel

Israel is the new name God gave the patriarch Jacob, meaning "he strives or persists with God."[3] Jacob's twelve sons became the forebears of the twelve tribes of Israel[4] and their descendants became known as the people of Israel.[5] After the exodus, when the Israelites arrived in the promised land, Canaan became known as the land of Israel.[6] When God established a monarchy, the land became known as the Kingdom of Israel.[7] After that kingdom split (930 BC), the ten northern tribes retained the name Israel.[8] In the New Testament, the term Israel is used both for the Jewish people (e.g., Rom. 11:7) and the land God promised the Jewish people (e.g., Matt. 2:20–21). Then, in 1948, when the Jewish people declared their independence in their ancient homeland, they called it "the State of Israel."[9] What makes all this confusing is that sometimes the word *Israel* is used as a stand-alone word for each of these definitions and it is only by the context of its usage that its meaning can be determined.

Jews/Jewish People

Today, the most common term used for the descendants of Abraham, Isaac, and Jacob is *Jews* or *the Jewish people*. This is derived from the Hebrew word *Judah*. How did this word group develop? The patriarch Jacob's fourth son was named Judah, and his descendants formed the tribe of Judah.[10] With the revolt of the ten northern tribes of Israel, the tribes of Judah and Benjamin united and formed the Kingdom of Judah.[11] When that kingdom fell to the Babylonian Empire in 586 BC, the people of Judah (Hebrew *Yehudah*) were exiled to Babylon, where they became united with the previously exiled people of the Northern Kingdom of Israel, and together they became known as "Jews" (Hebrew *Yehudim*).[12] After a seventy-year exile, King Cyrus allowed these Jewish captives to return to the land of Israel, which became known as "the land of the Jews." When the Romans gained control of the land of Israel, they renamed the Southern District *Judea*. After the Second Jewish Revolt against Rome (AD 132–35), the Roman Emperor Hadrian renamed the land "Palestine," after Israel's ancient enemies, the Philistines[13] in an attempt to sever the Jewish connection to their biblical homeland.

Zionism

The contemporary controversies over *Zionism* makes it essential to include this biblical word group. The etymology of the word "Zion" is unknown, but some have suggested it means stronghold and it referred to the original Jebusite city conquered by King David, who renamed the city "Jerusalem."[14] The Temple Mount came to be known in Scripture as Mount Zion but during the Byzantine period (AD 4th–7th centuries), Christian pilgrims misidentified the Western Hill of Jerusalem as Mount Zion.[15] In the Bible, the term *Zion* expanded from the Temple Mount to all of Jerusalem and even the whole land of Israel.[16] In the late nineteenth century, the Zionist movement arose among Jewish people scattered around the world, calling for the restoration of the Jewish people to their ancient homeland, Israel (then called Palestine). Today Zionism is merely the belief that Jewish people can rightfully exercise self-determination and have an autonomous state in their ancient homeland of Israel. It does not have any connection to racism, bigotry, or colonialism.[17]

Obviously, many of the terms mentioned above have their roots in Scripture and are commonly used in modern conversation relating to Jewish issues. As a result, Bible believers today have to discern what their relationship is to the modern State of Israel and to contemporary Jewish people. That is the topic we turn to next.

ISSUES AND ANSWERS

Biblical Israel/Modern Israel

Is modern Israel the same as biblical Israel?

Christians who believe the church has replaced ethnic Israel will often say that there is no correspondence between the two whatsoever. This belief is rooted in their view that Jesus is the true and perfect Israel. Therefore, the meaning of "Israel" expanded beyond ethnicity to include both Gentiles and Jews who have trusted in Jesus. As a result, those with this viewpoint see nothing distinctive or special about the Jewish people today or the modern State of Israel.

The problem with this position is that it ignores the clear biblical teaching that Israel refers to an ethnic people—the descendants of Abraham, Isaac, and Jacob. Both the Old and the New Testament affirm that, even in unbelief, ethnic Israel, or the Jewish people, retain their identity as God's chosen covenant people. For the sake of simplicity and clarity, let's choose just three passages to examine.

Romans 3:1–4. After discussing the advantages of being Jewish, namely, that God entrusted the Jewish people with the "oracles of God," Paul raises the question, "What then? If some did not believe, will their unbelief cancel God's faithfulness" (Rom. 3:3 HCSB)? He answers his rhetorical question emphatically, "Absolutely not! God must be true, even if everyone is a liar" (3:4 HCSB). The apostle's point is that even though most Jewish people—i.e., ethnic Israel—have not believed in their Messiah, God will still be faithful to His covenant promises to them.

Romans 9:4–5. In Romans 9:1–3, Paul expressed his heartfelt grief over ethnic Israel's unbelief in Jesus the Messiah. Then in verses 4–5, he affirms that despite the unbelief of Israel, the nation retains its distinctive national status. He states: "They are Israelites, and to them belong the adoption, the glory, the covenants, the giving of the law, the temple service, and the promises. The ancestors are theirs, and from them, by physical descent, came the Messiah, who is God over all, praised forever. Amen" (HCSB). The present tense verb in verse 4 demonstrates that all the benefits described still belong to Israel. As New Testament scholar Thomas Schreiner writes, "The present tense verb . . . (they are) indicates that the Jews still 'are' Israelites and that all the blessings named still belong to them."[18] Similarly, renowned Romans commentator Charles Cranfield concludes that Paul is saying that his fellow Jews, even though they do not believe in Jesus as the Messiah, remain "the chosen people of God."[19]

Romans 11:28–29. In these verses, Scripture affirms that despite Jewish opposition to the gospel, "from the standpoint of God's choice they are beloved for the sake of the fathers." Plainly, ethnic Israel has a distinctive national status despite their unbelief. Obviously, to experience forgiveness of sins, individual Jewish people, as do people of all backgrounds and ethnicities, need to trust that the Lord Jesus died and rose again for them. Nevertheless, the blessings listed in Romans 9:4 (see above) remain ethnic Israel's inheritance because "the gifts and the calling of God are irrevocable" (11:29).

So, how do the biblical kingdom of Israel and modern State of Israel correspond to each other? In some ways they are different: The biblical kingdom of Israel was a monarchy, and the modern State of Israel is a parliamentary democracy. Biblical Israel was a theocracy (governed by God), whereas modern Israel is a secular state.

The similarity lies in that the biblical kingdom of Israel was the nation-state of the Jewish people just as the modern secular State of Israel is the nation-state of the Jewish people. God gave the land covenant to the descendants of Abraham, Isaac, and Jacob (the Jewish people), granting them the land of Israel, and modern Jewish people retain title to that very same land. Furthermore, just as biblical Israel included Gentiles in their kingdom (think the mixed multitude leaving Egypt, Ruth the Moabitess, or Uriah the Hittite), so the modern State of Israel includes Arab Muslims, Armenian Christians, and other Gentiles. Calling Israel the nation-state of the Jewish people refers to it being predominantly a Jewish state (80 percent of the population) with equal rights for all citizens, even those who are not Jewish. Moreover, God promised to restore the Jewish people to their ancient homeland, and He fulfilled that prophecy after nearly two thousand years with the rebirth of the modern State of Israel, bringing the Jewish people home after suffering in exile for two millennia. (See the next chapter for a discussion of the land covenant and the prophetic promises of Israel's return.) In light of this relationship between biblical and modern Israel, what do we do with the biblical mandate to bless Israel?

Blessing for Blessing/Curse for Curse

In 2008, when the State of Israel initiated an operation in Gaza to respond to the terrorist group Hamas that had been launching rockets into civilian neighborhoods of Israel, a Chicago area pastoral prayer group, representing many churches, was meeting. One pastor present suggested that the group "pray for the peace of Jerusalem" (Ps. 122:6) to which another pastor asked, "Why?"

The first pastor expressed his commitment to bless Israel, taking it from Genesis 12:3: "And I will bless those who bless you, and the one who curses you I will curse." A lengthy discussion ensued about whether this verse referred to modern Jewish people or if it now applies to a "new Israel," composed of Jewish and Gentile believers in Jesus, namely the church.

Surely this was not the first time this very issue had come up, nor would it be the last time. In fact, every time there is a conflict involving Israel, some Jesus followers remain committed to blessing Israel, while others deny any relevance to contemporary Jewish people or the State of Israel. That is the issue before us now: Are Jesus followers called to bless Israel and the Jewish people, or is this principle no longer relevant?

A plain reading of Scripture will lead to the conclusion that this biblical standard refers directly to the Jewish people and as such, to Israel, as the Jewish state. Here is why. To begin, the blessing-for-blessing principle was given to Abraham as part of the Abrahamic covenant (Gen. 12:1–3) and reiterated to Jacob, as forefather of Israel and the recipient of the Abrahamic promises (Gen. 27:29).[20] Further, as mentioned in the previous section, Romans 9:1–5 refers to unbelieving Israel and nevertheless states that it is the "Israelites, to whom belongs . . . the covenants" (Rom. 9:4). Also, Romans 11:29 asserts concerning unbelieving Israel that "the gifts and the calling of God are irrevocable." If the Abrahamic covenant still belongs to the Jewish people as an irrevocable gift, then surely the blessing-for-blessing principle still pertains to the Jewish state.

The Lord Jesus Himself affirmed this principle when the Jewish leaders of Capernaum asked Him to heal a local centurion's servant. They asserted that "he is worthy for You to grant this to him; for he loves our nation and it was he who built us our synagogue" (Luke 7:4–5). Many English translations, including the New International Version and the New English Translation, correctly translate the next verse (v. 6) to say, "So Jesus went with them" indicating a resulting action. This gospel story is evidence that because the centurion had blessed the Jewish people, the Lord Jesus set out to bless him.

Does this mean that believers need to endorse every policy or action of the Israeli government? Obviously not. As citizens of a vibrant democracy, even Israelis do not always agree with the government themselves. What it does mean is that Jesus followers need to support Israel's legitimate right to exist and to defend itself. Furthermore, it is imperative that Christians take a stand against antisemitism[21] (the hatred of the Jewish people), including its newest form, hatred of the Jewish State of Israel.

Antisemitism, Old and New

Antisemitism, or the hatred of the Jewish people, is often called "the oldest hatred." Its roots go back to Pharoah's attempt to eliminate the Jewish people through the killing of their baby boys (Ex. 1:15–16). Bible readers are also aware of the book of Esther's record of Haman's attempt to commit genocide against the Jewish people in fifth century BC Persia. Throughout post-biblical Jewish history, Jewish people have been subject to slaughter at the hands of the Crusaders, the Inquisition, mob violence, and pogroms in Eastern Europe.

In the twentieth century, Adolf Hitler and the Nazi regime attempted to annihilate the Jewish people of Europe, succeeding at murdering six million. Among these were my four grandparents, two of my aunts and three of my uncles, my four half-brothers and one half-sister. It is this tragic history that has led to the Jewish saying, "So many Hamans but only one Purim" (the Jewish celebration of Haman's defeat, Esther 9:20–32). In other words, antisemitism will persist, yet the resilience of the Jewish people as celebrated in Purim, the commemoration of God's deliverance of the Jewish people during Esther's time, is ongoing.

After the Holocaust, it was presumed that antisemitism would be eradicated along with defeat of the Nazis. However, in recent years, particularly after the October 7, 2023, attack by Hamas on Israel, antisemitism has had a tremendous resurgence. The Anti-Defamation League has reported a 893 percent surge in antisemitic incidents in the United States in the years from 2015–2024.[22] Moreover, in 2024 alone, the year after Hamas attacked Israel, there were 9,354 antisemitic incidents in the United States, representing a 344 percent increase from the previous five years.[23] According to Oren Segal, ADL senior vice president for counter-extremism and intelligence, "This sustained elevation indicates the (post-Oct.7) experience was no temporary spike,"[24] reflecting a growing pattern of hatred of Jewish people and Israel becoming more acceptable in mainstream America. The extreme right and radical left both share in hatred of the Jews. Known as the "horseshoe effect," it indicates that despite their political differences, extremes on the right and left do agree on scapegoating and attacking Jewish people. What is the explanation for this irrational hatred?

Many claim both false and unjustifiable reasons for hatred, but from a biblical perspective there is a theological reason. Rooted in the words of Psalm 83, it declares the true source of antisemitism: hatred of the God of Israel motivates the hatred of the people of Israel. Note verses 2–5 specifically:

> For behold, **Your** enemies make an uproar, and those who hate **You** have exalted themselves. They make shrewd plans against

> **Your people**, and conspire together against **Your treasured ones**. They have said, "Come, and let us wipe them out as a nation, that the name of Israel will be remembered no more." For they have conspired together with one mind; against **You** they make a covenant.

Tragically, there are times when followers of Jesus the Messiah of Israel, who worship the very God of Israel of the Scriptures, have also joined in this ungodly hatred of His beloved people of Israel. Those of us who name the name of Jesus ought never to be part of this ungodly attitude and behavior. In fact, we who love the Lord Jesus, the Messiah of Israel, ought to be front and center in opposing the hatred of the Jewish people. When it comes to antisemitism, we need to remember the words of Proverbs 24:11–12:

> Deliver those who are being taken away to death, and those who are staggering to slaughter, Oh hold them back. If you say, "See, we did not know this," does He not consider it who weighs the hearts? And does He not know it who keeps your soul?

It is incumbent for believers to take our stand with God's beloved Jewish people and do all we can to resist this resurgent hatred of God's treasured ones.

A pastor I know who leads a Bible-believing church recently met with the all the rabbis of the local synagogues in his community. He expressed to them how disgusted he was with the return of antisemitism. He assured them that whenever there would be a march or a rally for the Jewish people, he and his congregation would be there. Furthermore, if ever any group threatened the synagogues, the Jewish schools, or the Jewish people in their community, he and his congregation pledged to stand up with them. He declared, "If anyone comes for you, they will have to go through us."

This is how all Christians need to respond to the return of antisemitism.

Anti-Zionism/Antisemitism

Some people object that they are not antisemitic but only opposed to the State of Israel—they are merely anti-Zionist. *New York Times* columnist Thomas Friedman addressed this attitude during the Palestinian War of Terror also known as the Second Intifada, writing,

> Criticizing Israel is not anti-Semitic, and saying so is vile. But singling out Israel for opprobrium and international sanction—out of all proportion to any other party in the Middle East—is anti-Semitic, and not saying so is dishonest.[25]

Israeli statesman and former Soviet dissident Natan Scharansky has offered a 3D test of antisemitism,[26] distinguishing between legitimate criticism of Israel and hatred of the Jewish state because it is Jewish. The first test is *delegitimization*, or denying the right of self-determination to the Jewish people in their own homeland.

Regardless of how much tension there is in the world, no other nation is constantly having its right to existence called into question.

The second test is *double standards*, or applying a standard to Israel's actions not expected of any other country in the Middle East or even a Western democracy. Where were the outcry and protests when Bashar Assad, at the time the dictator of Syria, had his soldiers kill 750,000 civilians in his own country? When the United States and Great Britain went to war with ISIS, the civilian collateral damage ratio was far greater than Palestinian deaths are in any of Israel's conflicts with Hamas, yet Israel is condemned. Of course, the death of any civilian is a tragic consequence of warfare, which should break our hearts. It is this concern that motivates Israel to take extraordinary measures to avoid civilian casualties, such as sending phone calls, text messages, and leaflets to Palestinian civilians, warning when and where Israeli troops will be operating.

The third test is *demonizatio*n, presuming Israel's actions are evil, without investigation. While engaging in a forum about Israel, a participant charged that Israel was dropping phosphorus bombs on Palestinians, allegedly proving Israeli malevolence toward Arab civilians. However, while it is true that Israel used phosphorus bombs, these were not dropped on civilians. Instead, Israel troops, in their desire to protect civilians, would search door to door for terrorists in Palestinian areas, endangering themselves by becoming easy targets for terrorist snipers. Therefore, the troops would roll a phosphorous device into the middle of the street (not on people) to create a cloud cover, protecting the Israeli troops from sniper fire. My fellow participant said he did not care about the reason for Israel's actions; they were just wrong. This is classic demonization, postulating and presuming Israel evil.

I would personally add a fourth test—*deceit*. An example would be what happens every time Israel engages in military self-defense. People will post social media pictures of suffering innocents from the Syrian civil war or the Lebanese civil war but attribute the photos to Israel's treatment of the Palestinians. Another instance of deception was early in Israel's war with Hamas after the Hamas invasion of Israel on October 7, 2023. Then terrorists reported to media outlets that Israel had rocketed a Palestinian hospital when in fact a Palestinian terrorist group's rocket, fired at Israel, fell short and landed on the hospital. Palestinian terrorist groups consistently manipulate the media via deceit and distortion and sadly, many news outlets accept the misinformation without proper investigation or confirmation of the facts.

In light of this, it is crucial for followers of Jesus not only to support the Jewish people, but also the Jewish State of Israel, resisting calls for boycotts, divestment, and sanctions (BDS). The BDS movement is designed to associate Israel wrongly with the racist behavior of the former South African apartheid government. It calls for governments and institutions to boycott Israeli businesses and academic institutions, divest from Israel economically, and sanction Israel as an outlaw state. The United States Department of State and many state and local governments have deemed the BDS movement as antisemitic. So much of the criticism of the State of Israel can be attributed to delegitimization, double standards, demonization, and deceit, that we should be compelled to fulfill the demand of the Abrahamic covenant and take our stand with the Jewish State.

CONCLUSION

In the late 1970s, the American Nazi Party, in a grotesque publicity stunt, sought permission to march in Skokie, Illinois, a Chicago suburb with the largest concentration of Holocaust survivors of any community in the United States at that time. The provocative behavior of these Neo-Nazis incensed Moody Bible Institute President, Dr. George Sweeting. He took out a page ad in major Chicago newspapers and published the following:

> Moody Bible Institute pledges to stand with the Jewish community. We want our Jewish friends to know that we pledge ourselves against any propaganda and activity which singles out Jewish people as their object of hatred. We commit ourselves to the pluralistic feature of our American society which honors every ethnic group, including our Jewish friends. Specifically do we pledge ourselves to the biblical position of God's choice of Israel for His holy Name's sake. The Scripture tells us, also, that the God of Abraham, Isaac and Jacob loves Israel with an unchanging,

> everlasting love. We owe so much to the very people from whom came the Messiah, the Prince of Peace. We proclaim that "No weapon formed against Israel will prosper."
>
> Moody Bible Institute issues an appeal to America and its leaders to remember the word concerning Abraham and his descendants, the covenant people of Israel, "I will bless those who bless you, and the one who curses you I will curse" (Gen. 12:3). We urge Christian leaders and layman to express their opposition to any action that would bring harm to the Jewish community in our nation.[27]

What Dr. Sweeting wrote then is just as true today. The ancient biblical promises made to the Jewish people are just as valid for modern Jewish people. God still has the same concern for the modern State of Israel as He did for the ancient nation of Israel. We would still urge Christians to act with care and concern for all Jewish people, those in our midst, around the world and in the State of Israel.

But what makes the Jewish people so significant in God's plan that we should care for them in this way? It is because God has established Israel and the Jewish people in the center of history and prophecy. So, it is to the crucial centrality of Israel in God's program that we turn next.

Chapter Two

ISRAEL IN THE CENTER OF HISTORY AND PROPHECY

How is it that one small group of people has had such an immense impact on society? The Jewish people comprise only one-fifth of 1 percent of the world's population, yet have won 22 percent of all the Nobel prizes awarded.[1] The entire world recognizes the achievements of Jewish notables such as Jonas Salk, who developed the polio vaccine; Albert Einstein, whose theory of relativity catapulted the world into the atomic age; and Sigmund Freud, who is the father of psychotherapy. People ask why the small State of Israel, which is about the size of the state of New Jersey, seems to have such a large role in world events, with news reports about it daily.

Certainly, Jewish people have had and will continue to have a profound influence on the world because of God's choice of Israel to be His people. By examining God's Word, it is possible to understand what is happening in the news today and what will take place in the future. The best place to start doing that is by looking at the past—when God called Israel to be His chosen people.

ISRAEL'S PAST

The unconditional covenants that God made with Israel in the past are foundational for understanding Israel's importance in the prophetic future. These covenants with Israel govern our understanding of the Jewish people and form the backbone of biblical prophecy.

The Abrahamic Covenant

Genesis 12:1–3 records God's call of Abraham out of Ur of the Chaldees (Babylon) and the specific promises He made to him. These promises were confirmed and clarified in later passages of Genesis (13:14–17; 15:1–7; 17:1–21). Additionally, they were reconfirmed to Abraham's son Isaac (26:3–4) and grandson Jacob (28:13–15), identifying which line of Abraham would receive God's promises.

The promises God made to Abraham fell into three categories: personal, national, and universal.[2] Particularly notable is the *national* promise: Abraham's descendants would multiply and be "as numerous as the stars in the sky and as the sand on the seashore" (Gen. 22:17 NIV) and that God would give Abraham and his people the land of Canaan as their "everlasting possession" (17:8), with its boundaries extending from the river of Egypt in the west to the Euphrates River in the east and the land of the Hittites in the north (15:18–21).

This is interesting in light of all the contemporary questions about ownership of the land of Israel today. Regardless of the political disputes, God has granted the title deed of the land of Israel to the Jewish people. At present, this land promise has not been fulfilled in its entirety but will be when the Messiah Jesus returns and establishes His kingdom on earth.

The national promises also gave Israel a unique position as God's barometer of blessing: Those nations that would bless Israel would be blessed and those that cursed Israel would be cursed (12:3; 27:29). This principle applied during Abraham's life (12:10–20; 14:12–20; 26:1–11) and throughout the history of the Jewish people (Deut. 14:1–2; 30:7). Significantly, this will be the principle that guides God's judgment of the Gentile nations when Jesus returns. The sheep and the goats will be divided on the basis of their treatment of Jesus' physical brothers and sisters, the Jewish people. That is why He will say, "Whatever you did for one of the least of these brothers of mine, you did for me" (Matt. 25:40). Regarding the *universal* aspects of the Abrahamic covenant—that God promised to bless the whole world through

Abraham's descendants, or "seed" (Gen. 22:18)—the ultimate fulfillment of this promise occurred through the ministry of Jesus the Messiah of Israel. Through His death and resurrection, Messiah Jesus provided atonement for the whole world (Gal. 3:16).

The Other Covenants

The Land Covenant. Later biblical covenants expanded three particular aspects of the Abrahamic covenant, namely its promises of the land, the seed, and the blessing. For example, the land promise was expanded into the land covenant[3] found in Deuteronomy 28–30. This promise assured that the people of Israel would experience physical and material blessing from God if they would obey His Law. It also assured Israel that God would discipline the nation for persistent disobedience and idolatry by driving the people out of the land and into exile. God also promised to restore the Jewish people to their land after much suffering. Both their suffering and restoration are said to occur "in the latter days" (Deut. 4:30; 31:29).

The Davidic Covenant. God's promise of seed for Abraham was further expanded in the Davidic covenant. This covenant is foundational for the messianic hope of the Hebrew Bible and the basis of the New Testament expectation of a future kingdom. When David wanted to build a house for God (a temple), instead God promised David that *He* would build a house for David (2 Sam. 7:8–16). God affirmed that He would give David an eternal dynasty and kingdom with an eternal ruler to sit on David's throne (v. 16). That ruler was to be one of David's sons (his seed) who was also to have a Father/Son relationship with God (vv. 12–16). That this would have a messianic fulfillment is made clear in 2 Samuel 7:19 (HCSB), where David responds to the covenant by saying, "You have also spoken about Your servant's house *in the distant future*. And this is a revelation for mankind, O Lord GOD."

This messianic element is developed in the narrative of 1 and 2 Kings. There, it initially appears that the promise would be fulfilled through David's son Solomon. In fact, since Solomon even believed that he was the potential fulfillment, he built the temple. But the Lord warned Solomon that the promise would be fulfilled through him only if he would "walk in My statutes and execute My ordinances and keep all My commandments by walking in them" (1 Kings 6:12). The author of 1 Kings quickly points out how miserably Solomon failed to obey God with his marriages to foreign women who turned his heart away from God (1 Kings 11:1–4). In fact, no Davidic king succeeded in obeying God completely but all—even the good ones—ended with failure.

Thus, the book of 2 Kings ends with the temple destroyed and the Davidic dynasty in ruins. What remained was the hope and expectation that God would one day send an eternal ruler who would build the true temple of God and sit on the throne of David. The prophet Zechariah foretold that this future King would come to unite the office of priest and king and build the temple of the Lord (Zech. 6:9–15).

The hope and longing for this Son of David consumed the prophets, from Isaiah to Amos,[4] and found its fulfillment in the birth of Jesus. The angel Gabriel announced His birth, saying, "The Lord God will give Him the throne of His father David; and He will reign over the house of Jacob forever, and His kingdom will have no end" (Luke 1:32–33). Jesus was the Promised One, the Son of David and the Son of God. He announced the coming of God's kingdom, and He will return to rule from the literal throne of David in Jerusalem and establish the kingdom of God on earth.

The New Covenant. The blessing component of the Abrahamic covenant was amplified by the new covenant. The term "new covenant" comes from Jeremiah 31:31–34, but it had already been promised by Moses (Deut. 30:1–14) and would be affirmed in other prophets (Ezek. 36:26–27). The newness of this covenant is derived from its distinction from the old covenant, the laws given by God on Mount Sinai. In Jeremiah 31:32, God promised that the new covenant would be unlike the old covenant He gave Israel after the nation left Egypt. This old covenant is an obvious reference to the Sinai covenant, not the Abrahamic covenant or any other covenant. Hebrews 8:13 confirms this when it states that the old covenant (the Sinai covenant) has been made obsolete by the establishment of the new covenant.

The new covenant was promised to Israel and Judah and

ratified through the death and resurrection of Jesus the Messiah (Matt. 26:27–28). The new covenant was indeed inaugurated with Israel through the righteous remnant of Jewish people who believe in Jesus as Messiah. Today, the church, composed of Jewish and Gentile followers of Jesus, shares those spiritual blessings through its relationship with the Messiah Jesus. However, only when Messiah returns and begins His kingdom will He establish the new covenant in its fullest sense. In that day, when everyone knows the Lord, all people will fully experience this universal aspect of the Abrahamic covenant.

Since God keeps His promises, these covenants from Israel's past remain significant for her present and future. The land aspect of the Abrahamic covenant reaffirms that the title deed to the land of Israel belongs to the Jewish people, and the covenant assures that there will be a future kingdom that will include all the land God promised—something which throughout her long history, Israel has never possessed. The Davidic covenant assures that Jesus the Messiah, the Son of David, will return and establish His kingdom on earth. He will rule from David's throne as the righteous King of Israel and sovereign of the world. Finally, the new covenant guarantees that there will be a time when all Israel will turn to her Messiah. Then Israel and all the nations of the world will know the Lord.

These covenants certainly give hope for the future, but what of Israel today?

ISRAEL'S PRESENT

Since these covenants are all from Israel's past, some people have improperly taken them away from Israel and applied them to the church today. It is true that the vast majority of Jewish people have failed to recognize Jesus as their Messiah. This rejection has motivated some sincere followers of Christ to adopt the erroneous opinion that Israel's promises have transferred to the church. Their approach seems to take a rather shortsighted view of the faithfulness of God.

One of the essential principles of the Abrahamic covenant is that it is unconditional and eternal. Abraham did not need to do anything to receive or maintain this covenant. Furthermore, when God reaffirmed His covenant with Abraham, He solemnized His divine oath with the offering of sacrifices (Gen. 15:8–17). In ancient times, when two parties wanted to bind themselves to a covenant, they would lay the severed parts of a sacrificial animal on the ground, and both parties would walk in their midst. This signified that both were in agreement and bound by the covenant. When God solemnized His oath to Abraham, He deliberately excluded Abraham from the process. Instead, God caused Abraham to fall into a deep sleep and God alone passed through the animal parts. This demonstrated that God was solely responsible for this covenant—it did not depend on Abraham or his descendants but on God alone. In light of the unconditional nature of the Abrahamic covenant, there are several truths about the Jewish people today that must be maintained.

Israel as God's Chosen People

God has retained Israel as His chosen people. This is not only an Old Testament concept; the New Testament agrees with it as well. Paul wrote that despite Israel's disbelief in Jesus, "God has not rejected His people whom He foreknew" (Rom. 11:2). Moreover, although most Jewish people have rejected the good news of Jesus, the people of Israel remain God's beloved chosen people "for the sake of the fathers" (11:28)—a clear reference to the Abrahamic covenant. Paul categorically states that God's gifts and call to Israel are irrevocable (11:29).

Remaining God's chosen people does not mean that Jewish people have forgiveness and a personal relationship with God apart from faith in their Messiah Jesus. Jewish people, as all people, must trust in Jesus. Regardless, the Lord's words in Deuteronomy 14:2 remain true as ever: "the LORD has chosen you to be a people for His own possession out of all the peoples who are on the face of the earth." God did this not because of any merit found in the Jewish people. God told Israel that He chose them "because the LORD loved you and kept the oath which He swore to your forefathers" (Deut. 7:8). Since God is faithful to His promises and loyal in His love, the Jewish people are still the chosen people.

A Preserved and Protected People

God is active today preserving and protecting the Jewish people. Through the prophet Jeremiah, the Lord assures that it will be impossible ever to destroy the Jewish people. In fact, in order to put an end to the Jewish people, it would be necessary to stop the sun, moon, and stars from shining. God declares that only if these impossible acts could be accomplished will "the offspring of Israel . . . cease from being a nation before Me." He further states that if the heavens and foundations of the earth could be measured, only then would I "cast off all the offspring of Israel" (Jer. 31:35–37). Plainly, the Lord will preserve His people. That is why the prophet Zechariah says of the people of Israel that whoever touches them "touches the apple of His eye" (Zech. 2:8).

Throughout history there have been those who have sought Israel's destruction—from Haman to Hitler to Saddam Hussein to the ayatollahs of Iran—but they have never succeeded. In 1981, I attended the World Gathering of Holocaust Survivors in Jerusalem, as a second-generation participant. There I heard Menachem Begin, the late prime minister of Israel, declare before those Holocaust survivors and their children that Hitler's attempt to annihilate the Jewish people ought not to cause them to doubt God's existence but rather to believe in Him. Begin said that apart from God's providential intervention, there was no way Hitler could have failed. The prime minister recognized that God was true to His promise to preserve and ultimately to protect His chosen people.

Frederick the Great, monarch of Prussia (1740–1786), is said to have asked his chaplain for one clear and compelling evidence for the existence of God. The chaplain replied: "The amazing Jew, your Majesty."

The preservation of the Jewish people, despite a history of hatred and persecution, has led historian Paul Johnson to call the Jews "the most tenacious people in history."[5] It is far better to say that the Jewish people are protected by the tenacious God of history, who is faithful to His promises and relentless in preserving His people. For this reason, no weapon formed against Israel will ever prosper (Isa. 54:17).

A Remnant Being Saved

God is presently saving a remnant of Israel. Paul asserted, in Romans 11:1–5, that God did not reject the Jewish people, and as proof he offered the doctrine of the remnant. His point was that God has always worked through a faithful remnant both during the Old Testament and the present age. Even though the vast majority of the Jewish people have rejected Jesus as the Messiah, God in His faithfulness has preserved a remnant within Israel, chosen by grace, who would believe. So Paul wrote, "There has also come to be at the present time a remnant according to God's gracious choice" (v. 5).

Throughout the entire church age there has always been a remnant of Jewish people who have sincerely believed in Jesus as their Messiah and Lord. Since 1967, a significant number of Jewish people have come to believe in Jesus and still maintain their unique role as the Jewish remnant. There are at least 250,000 messianic Jews worldwide, with some estimating numbers as high as 1.3 million, participating in hundreds of messianic congregations and in many evangelical churches around the globe. This movement is especially evident in North America, Europe, South America, Russia, Ukraine, and other countries of the former Soviet Union, as well as Israel.

Paul anticipated a day when the remnant would become the whole. He wrote in Romans 11:25–26 that at Jesus' return, when the full number of Gentiles have come in, Israel as a whole will turn in faith to Jesus as their Messiah, "and so all Israel will be saved." Perhaps the Spirit of God's unique move among the Jewish people today is a precursor to the far greater movement that will take place yet in the future.

Restored to the Land

God is restoring the Jewish people to the land of Israel. Since their exile around the world nearly two millennia ago, Jewish people have daily prayed that they would be restored to the land of Israel. The Hebrew prophets foretold a day when God would draw His people back to their promised land. Throughout church history, Christians for the most part could not conceive of a literal fulfillment of this promise, so they interpreted it figuratively. However, some believers in the nineteenth century did indeed take the promise of a return literally and therefore began to anticipate a Jewish return to the land of Israel.

This modern return began with the nineteenth century "Lovers of Zion," who believed that a return to the land of Israel was the only hope for Jewish people to survive in a world filled with anti-Jewish hatred. It expanded with Theodore Herzl and the rise of Zionism, leading to the five immigration waves known as *aliyot* and the issuing of the Balfour Declaration (1917) that advocated a Jewish national home in their biblical homeland in what was then called Palestine.

After the birth of the State of Israel came "the ingathering of the exiles," both Holocaust survivors and 750,000 Jewish people expelled from Arab countries opposed to Israel. A major wave of Jewish people returning to their homeland took place with the fall of the Soviet Union, releasing 1.5 million Jewish people from exile and bringing them home to the land of Israel. In the first quarter of the twenty-first century, with heightened antisemitism in France, nearly 50,000 French Jews have made their home in Israel.

The State of Israel: A Fulfillment of Bible Prophecy

Bible believers frequently ask how the unprecedented reborn State of Israel fits with Bible prophecy. For several reasons, it appears that the best explanation is that the modern State of Israel seems to be a dramatic work of God in fulfillment of the Bible's predictions of a Jewish return to the land of Israel.

First, the Bible predicts that Israel would return to her land in unbelief. Biblical prophecy indicates that the Jewish people will turn to God only *afte*r returning to the land of Israel. Ezekiel 36:24 says, "For I will take you from the nations, gather you from all the lands and bring you into your own land." The next two verses (25–26) continue, "*Then* I will sprinkle clean water on you, and you will be clean; I will cleanse you from all your filthiness and from all your idols. Moreover, I will give you a new heart and put a new spirit within you; and I will remove the heart of stone from your flesh and give you a heart of flesh."

Note that the *national* restoration of the Jewish people will precede the spiritual regeneration of Israel. Israel has been reborn as a secular state by secular Jews. This is the precursor to the day when the entire nation turns in faith to Jesus Messiah Yeshua.

Second, the Bible predicts that Israel would return to her land in stages. Ezekiel 37 contains the vision of a valley of dry bones. The bones come to life in stages: first sinews on the bones, then flesh, then skin, and, finally, the breath of life (vv. 6–10). Then God told Ezekiel that "these bones are the whole house of Israel" (v. 11) and that their restoration is a picture of the way God will bring them "into the land of Israel" (v. 12). So the regathering of Israel is not an event that will occur in one fell swoop. Rather, it is a process that culminates in the nation receiving the breath of life by turning to their Messiah.

This is precisely how the Jewish people have returned to the land. Through the different *aliyot* (immigration waves), beginning in 1882 to the immigrants from the former Soviet Union in the 1990s, the Jewish people have returned in stages. The final step will be when the entire nation turns in faith to Jesus their Messiah and God breathes the breath of life on them.

Third, the Bible predicts that Israel would return to her land through persecution. God says of Israel through the prophet Jeremiah, "I will restore them to their own land which I gave to their fathers" (16:15). In the next verse, God says that He will use "fishermen" and "hunters" to pursue His people back to their land (v. 16). This metaphor for persecution has been literally fulfilled in the rebirth of Israel. Since the birth of modern Zionism, the primary motivation for return to the land of Israel has been anti-Jewish persecution. In the past 140 years, God has used czarist pogroms, Polish economic discrimination, Nazi genocide, Arab hatred, and Soviet repression to drive Jewish people back to their homeland. Economic success and religious freedom in the Diaspora keep Jewish people complacent about returning, so God uses "fishermen" and "hunters" to drive them back to the promised land.

Fourth, the Bible predicts that Israel would return to her land to set the stage for end-time events. Daniel 9:27 speaks of a firm covenant between the future world dictator and the Jewish people, which will unleash the final events before Messiah Jesus' return. This prophecy assumes a reborn State of Israel. The Jewish state had to be restored so this prediction (and many others) could take place. A reborn State of Israel is necessary for this treaty/covenant to be signed, for the temple to be rebuilt, for Jerusalem to be surrounded by the nations during the campaign of Armageddon, even for the Messiah Jesus to return to deliver the Jewish people from their enemies. Since Israel has returned in unbelief, in stages, through persecution, it is likely that the modern State of Israel fulfills the predictions of the ancient Hebrew prophets . . . and sets the stage for events yet to come.

God established His plan for Israel in the ancient past by establishing His covenants with the Jewish people. On the basis of these covenants, God continues to work among the Jewish people in the present age. But God has much more in store for Israel in the future. In fact, He has given the Jewish people a featured role to play in the outworking of end-time events.

ISRAEL'S FUTURE

Throughout history, God has caused the Jewish people to have an influence that far outweighs their size. Their influence will be even greater in the future. During the end times, Israel will be the focal point in God's future program in several ways.

A Role in the Future Tribulation

Israel will play a vital role in starting the future tribulation. Although the Bible teaches that the Lord Jesus can return for His church at any moment (Matt. 25:1–13; 1 Thess. 4:13–18;

5:1–11), it gives a specific requirement for the beginning of the future tribulation period. The tribulation will begin only when Israel signs a covenant (a treaty of some sort) with the future false messiah. According to Daniel 9:27, the seventieth "week" (a period of seven years) of Daniel's vision begins when "he will make a firm covenant with the many for one week." The identity of the "he" in this verse, according to the rest of the verse, is a future world ruler who will set up an abomination in a yet to be built temple. This ruler is frequently called the "Antichrist" or the "Man of Sin," but I prefer to call him the "future false messiah."

This false messiah will make a covenant or treaty with *many*. From the context, it appears that many refers either to many in Israel or to Israel and her neighbors. This treaty, either between Israel and the false messiah or Israel and her neighbors but brokered by the false messiah, will most likely establish peace in the Middle East for the first half of the tribulation (three and one-half years). But the false messiah will then break the covenant and unleash hell on earth, culminating in the campaign of Armageddon.

Significantly, the Messiah, Jesus, can return for the church at *any* time—even as you read this paragraph. However, the tribulation will only begin when Israel and the future false messiah will make a treaty together—showing Israel's vital role as a catalyst for the tribulation period. Besides starting the tribulation, Israel is crucial for other aspects of future events.

A Focal Point of the Tribulation

Israel will be the focus of the tribulation. The prophet Jeremiah clarifies this when he calls the tribulation period the "time of Jacob's distress" (30:7). The name "Jacob" refers in this context not to the patriarch but the people who descended from him. Israel is God's primary concern during the tribulation, since the church will already have been removed at the rapture (when Jesus instantly calls His followers into heaven [1 Thess. 4:13–17]).

Israel's central place in the tribulation is evident in several ways. First, Israel will face *persecution* during the tribulation. In Revelation 12, God describes Satan's activity at both the Messiah's first and second comings. He uses the figure of "a woman clothed with the sun, and the moon under her feet, and on her head a crown of twelve stars" (12:1). In light of Joseph's dream (Gen. 37:9), it is best to understand the woman as a reference to Israel. The woman (Israel) gave birth to a Son (Jesus, the messianic King), who was persecuted by the dragon (Satan) at His birth (Rev. 12:1–6). This happened at Jesus' first coming through the attempt by Herod the Great to destroy the rightful King of the Jewish people with the slaughter of the innocent (Matt. 2:13–18).

Prior to the second coming of the Messiah, the dragon will be cast to the earth and he will begin to persecute "the woman who gave birth to the male child" (Rev. 12:13), namely, Israel. Not only will the dragon be "enraged with the woman" (Israel) but he will make war "with the rest of her children" (Rev. 12:17).

This refers to the future satanic attack on both the nation and the remnant of Israel who will come to faith during the tribulation. During this time the Jewish people will endure unprecedented hatred and persecution.

Second, the people of Israel will experience *cleansing* during the tribulation. God will permit the suffering of His chosen people in order to discipline them so that they will turn to Messiah Jesus in faith. The prophet Ezekiel speaks of the tribulation as the time when Israel passes under God's rod of discipline (Ezek. 20:37). This discipline will result in Israel being purged of rebels (those who have not yet trusted in Jesus as their Messiah) and the rest of the nation being brought into the bond of the covenant (Ezek. 20:37–38). The prophet Jeremiah records God's purpose for the tribulation when God says to Israel, "I will chasten you justly" (Jer. 30:11). According to Zechariah, God will discipline the people of Israel in order to "refine them as silver is refined, and test them as gold is tested." As a result, Israel will call on God's name and He will answer them saying, "'They are My people,' and they will say, 'The LORD is my God'" (Zech. 13:9). God will use the suffering of the Jewish people to discipline them so that they will come to know the Lord through Jesus their Messiah.

Third, during the tribulation many in Israel will devote themselves in *service* to God. Revelation 7:3–4 describes 144,000 Jewish people, from all the twelve tribes, who are called "the bond-servants of our God." They are Jewish people who come to faith in Jesus after the Lord snatches the church into His presence at the rapture. No doubt there will be Bibles and other materials that will enable these 144,000 Jewish people to understand and receive the gospel. This remnant of Israel will be sealed by God and set apart for His service. What they will do in service to God is unclear. Perhaps they will be the evangelists of the tribulation period, helping people all over the world put their trust in Jesus the Messiah, even during the tribulation.

Fourth, Israel will face *war* during the tribulation. At the culmination of the tribulation, world leaders will gather their armies in northern Israel, next to Mount Megiddo, to begin the campaign of Armageddon (Rev. 16:16). These nations will march on Jerusalem and besiege the Jewish people; there attacking armies of the world will fight against Jerusalem, capture and ransack the city, and commit horrible atrocities (Zech. 12:2–3; 14:2). God will allow this so that Israel will turn to Him and then be saved. The tribulation will be a time of war for the Jewish people.

God's wrath will fall on the earth during the Tribulation period. It will be a time of suffering for all peoples. But more than any other nation, God will focus His attention on the Jewish people, with the goal of bringing them to faith in their Messiah Jesus and restoring them to Himself. Besides Israel's importance in starting and being the focus of the tribulation, the nation will play an even more significant role in the second coming of Jesus the Messiah.

An Initiator in the Messiah's Return

Israel will initiate the second coming of the Messiah. Although no one knows the day or hour of Jesus' return for His church, we do know that He will return at the conclusion of the seven-year tribulation period. What will bring about the end of that period and return the Messiah to the earth? The Scriptures teach that it will be the nation of Israel who will call for Jesus to return, and He will do so in His mercy.

Matthew 23:37–39 contains Jesus' response to Israel's national rejection of Him. He would have longed to gather Israel as a mother hen gathers her chicks, He said, but when the leadership of Israel rejected Jesus, they made that impossible. Therefore, Jesus prophesied, Jerusalem and the temple would be destroyed. However, He did offer Israel hope in the midst of this sad prediction. "For I say to you, from now on you will not see Me until you say, 'Blessed is He who comes in the name of the LORD!'" (Matt. 23:39). The Lord Jesus requires Israel to say these traditional Hebrew words of welcome and reception. In effect, Jesus is saying that He will not return to Israel until they welcome Him as the Messiah. What will cause Israel to do this?

The prophet Zechariah predicted that at the end of the tribulation the nations will gather in Israel and attack Jerusalem (Zech. 12:1–9). The suffering will have been so severe and the situation so grave that Israel's leaders will turn to God for deliverance. God will graciously open their eyes so that "they will look on Me whom they have pierced; and they will mourn for Him, as one mourns for an only son" (12:10). Israel will mourn for all the years that they had rejected Jesus. The Messiah will return and "a fountain will be opened for the house of David and for the inhabitants of Jerusalem, for sin and for impurity" (13:1). Then, as Paul had foretold, all the Jewish people alive in that day will put their faith in Jesus as their Messiah, "and so all Israel will be saved" (Rom. 11:26).

Not only will the Lord deliver them from their sin, He will also deliver them from their attackers. According to Zechariah, "Then the LORD will go forth and fight against those nations, as when He fights on the day of battle. In that day His feet will stand on the Mount of Olives. . . . Then the LORD, my God, will come and all the holy ones with Him!" (14:3–5). It is only when Israel calls for Messiah Jesus to return and looks to Him in faith, that He will return. Israel is the key to the second coming of Jesus the Messiah. Even after the Messiah Jesus returns, Israel will still have a crucial position in God's program.

A Special Place in the Messiah's Kingdom

Israel will be the head of the nations in the messianic kingdom. The messianic kingdom that King Jesus will establish will have many marvelous components. From the renovation of the earth to universal peace, it will be a glorious time. But for Israel, it will be remarkable. All Jewish people will have turned to their Messiah

Jesus whom they will now know as Lord. Those who are still scattered around the world will be returned to the land of Israel and will fully inhabit the land according to the provisions of the Abrahamic covenant.

The Messiah Jesus will begin His reign from the throne of David in Jerusalem and will rule over Israel and all the nations. Significantly, Israel will be the head of the nations then, even as the book of Deuteronomy had foretold: "The LORD will make you the head and not the tail" (28:13). Isaiah promised that God would again choose Israel and settle them in their land. Then the house of Israel will possess the nations (Isa. 14:1–2).

Although many biblical passages speak of Israel's leadership of the Gentile nations in the messianic kingdom (Isa. 49:22–23; 60:1–3; 61:4–9; Mic. 7:14–17; Zeph. 3:20), one is especially notable in that it speaks of the spiritual influence Israel will have over the nations. The Lord Almighty Himself describes the scene when "many peoples and mighty nations will come" to worship Him in Jerusalem. "In those days ten men from all the nations will grasp the garment of a Jew saying, 'Let us go with you, for we have heard that God is with you'" (Zech. 8:22–23).

When the Jewish people know the Lord, He will give them great influence, and they will lead the Gentile nations in worship of Him. This small nation of Israel will continue to have a large impact, even in the messianic kingdom. The ancient rabbis were right when they said, "Israel is like a vine: trodden underfoot; but some time later its wine is placed on the table of a king. So, Israel, at first oppressed, will eventually come to greatness."[6]

THE "IMMORTAL" JEW

Mark Twain wrote, "All things are mortal but the Jew; all other forces pass, but he remains. What is the secret of his immortality?"[7] Twain has asked the right question. What is the secret of this special people? At the outset of this chapter, we asked the same question. The answer, as we have seen, lies in the Abrahamic covenant. Long ago, God, in His grace, chose Israel to be His special people. Therefore, even now, in the present age, Israel remains God's chosen people, the special object of His love and concern. Since this is true, God will be faithful to all the promises that He made to Abraham, Isaac, and Jacob.

Despite all this strong evidence of God's faithfulness to His people Israel, there are many followers of Jesus who believe God has transferred His promises to the church. Has the church replaced Israel in God's plan and program? This is the crucial question that must now be answered.

Chapter Three

CORRECTING SPIRITUAL IDENTITY THEFT

We live in an age of identity theft. Whether it's email or text messages, I receive a steady stream of invitations offering me an unexpected inheritance or fortune. All I have to do is send my Social Security number, bank account, or credit card numbers and I will be sure to make a mint. Of course, I know the goal of these offers is to steal my identity and take my money.

Even more distressing, there is a long tradition in the church to engage in something similar—spiritual identity theft.

Since the second century, the predominant view within the church has been that God has rejected His people and transferred His promises from Israel to the church. Some have called this replacement theology, meaning that the church has *replaced* Israel in God's program. Others have called it supersessionism, indicating that the church has *superseded* the Jewish people as God's chosen people.

After the Holocaust, many in the church understood that replacement theology lay at the heart of Christian passivity in resisting Nazism. Therefore, those who hold these views sometimes seek to soften the terms and call it expansion or fulfillment theology. This teaching is no different than replacement theology, but it sounds less aggressive to say God has expanded or fulfilled Israel to include both Jewish and Gentile followers of Jesus (meaning the church), as opposed to understanding Israel to refer exclusively to ethnic Jewish people.

But is this true? Was spiritual identity theft actually part of God's plan and program?

In the last chapter, we examined an overview of God's promises to ethnic Israel in the past, His plan for Jewish people at present, and His program for them in the future. Yet we may wonder, where does the church fit in regarding all this? It is clear in Scripture that the church and Israel are distinct from each other. Recognizing the differences between Israel and the church is a way to overcome the church's spiritual identity theft of the Jewish people. In this chapter, we will examine how Israel and the church are distinct.

DIFFERENT BEGINNINGS

The first way to see that Israel and the church are distinct is by recognizing their different beginnings. Israel traces its inception to the call of Abraham and God's covenantal promise to make a people out of Abraham's descendants (Gen. 12:2; 15:3–5). Furthermore, this promise was passed on to Isaac and Jacob/Israel (26:3–5; 35:11–12) and the twelve sons of Jacob (46:8–27). Then, the descendants of these sons became known as the people of Israel. Thus, the biblical definition of Israel is purely ethnic, referring to the descendants of Abraham, Isaac, and Jacob, and Jacob's twelve sons.

The church did not begin at the same time as the Jewish people. For example, in Matthew 16:18, the Lord Jesus promised "I will build My church," indicating that the church was yet future and not yet in existence during His earthly ministry. Clearly, the Lord Jesus saw the church as distinct from Israel, which was already in existence when He made that promise.

A simple reading of Acts also shows that the events at Pentecost in Acts 2, with the giving of the Holy Spirit, refer to the birthday of the church. Although Acts 2 does not explicitly state this, later in Acts 10–11, it is made plain. After Peter preached to Cornelius and his household and they believed, Peter baptized them (Acts 10:1–48). He later had to explain his baptism of these Gentiles who believed in Jesus the Messiah without first requiring them to be circumcised and thereby adopt Judaism (Acts 11:1–18). Peter explained that "the Holy Spirit fell upon them just as He did upon us *at the beginning*" (Acts 11:15). Obviously, Peter was referring to the way the Holy Spirit had previously fallen on the apostles at Pentecost, an event he labels as "the beginning." By this, Peter could only be referring to the beginning of the church. The New Testament sees the beginning of the church as distinct from the patriarchal beginnings of Israel.

DIFFERENT COMMUNITIES

A second way to see the distinctions between Israel and the church is that the two groups are composed of different people. As shown above, the Hebrew Bible had already defined Israel as the physical descendants of Abraham, Isaac, and Jacob. Although the Scriptures distinguished between national Israel and the faithful remnant of believers within the nation (see 1 Kings 19:18), Israel as a nation was always composed of the physical descendants of Abraham, Isaac, and Jacob.

The Remnant—Romans 11:1–5. One New Testament passage that clearly affirms an ethnic definition of Israel is Romans 11:1–5. Paul's first assertion in this text is that God has not rejected His people Israel, despite their unbelief in Jesus the Messiah (Rom. 11:1). Second, as proof of God's faithfulness to ethnic Israel, Paul maintains that there is a faithful remnant of believers within Israel. In fact, Paul argues that there always was a faithful remnant within ethnic Israel, as seen in the "seven thousand men who have not bowed the knee to Baal" in Elijah's day (Rom. 11:4). He concludes that there is and always will be a faithful remnant of Jewish followers of Jesus, "a remnant according to God's gracious choice" (v. 5). Clearly, Paul holds to the ethnic definition of Israel as descendants of Abraham, Isaac, and Jacob. Moreover, the proof that this definition will not change is found in God's choice for salvation of the remnant of Israel, the Jewish believers in Jesus.

True Jews—Romans 2:28–29. Many evangelical interpreters in the modern past held to a supersessionist viewpoint and referred to Romans 2:28–29 as evidence that Paul had redefined the term "Jew" to refer not to ethnically Jewish people but to the church, composed of Jewish and Gentile believers in Jesus. In these verses, Paul identified a Jewish person as not one who is a Jew "outwardly" (physical circumcision alone) but one who is a Jew "inwardly" with circumcision "of the heart." They assumed Paul to be redefining and expanding Jewish people—from the physical descendants of Abraham, Isaac, and Jacob—to the spiritual followers of the Messiah Jesus, especially Gentile believers.

However, since the second half of the twentieth century, most evangelical New Testament scholars have come to understand Paul to be speaking only of Jewish believers in Jesus as the truest Jews because this fits the context best. In Romans 1:18–3:20, Paul is making the case that all people are sinful. He begins by showing that pagan Gentiles are lost in sin (1:18–32) and then proceeds to demonstrate that even Gentile moralists are separated from God by their sin (2:1–16). Having proven the sinfulness of Gentiles, Paul asserts that Jewish people are also sinful (2:17–3:8) as is all the world (3:9–20).

The discussion of the meaning of true Jewishness (2:28–29) falls right in the section about Jewish people. Paul is not talking about Gentile believers becoming true Jews. Rather, he is defining those who are the truest Jews within the Jewish community. This is not an expansion of the meaning of "Jew" but a narrowing of it. Specifically, Paul is referring to Jewish people who believe in Messiah Jesus as the truest Jews.[1] These faithful Jewish people are the remnant among the whole people of Israel. Therefore, even here, the word "Jew" refers to ethnic Jewish people.

Besides the near context, the biblical context also supports this view. The idea of the truest Jews being those who are both physically and spiritually circumcised is also found in the Old Testament (Lev. 26:41; Deut. 10:16; 30:6). Later in the Hebrew Bible, the prophet Jeremiah instructs Israel to "circumcise yourselves to the LORD and remove the foreskins of your heart" (Jer. 4:4). He also warns Israel that those who are merely physically circumcised but not spiritually circumcised will one day face punishment (Jer. 6:10–12). He laments that "all the house of Israel are uncircumcised of heart" (Jer. 9:26). Jeremiah has recognized that there is a group of Jews within the Jewish community who have circumcised both their flesh and their hearts. They are ethnic Jewish people with a true faith and devotion to the God of Israel. They are the truest Jews. Clearly, Paul is adopting the same perspective.

Michael Vanlaningham accurately notes that in Romans 2:28–29, "Paul is speaking only of true, believing Jews. . . . Gentile believers are not in view, and the idea that Gentile Christians are the new Israel is foreign to this section."[2] All this is not to say that Paul meant that Jewish people who do not believe in Jesus, were no longer to be considered actual Jewish people. In the very next verse (Rom. 3:1), speaking of Jews who do not believe, Paul asks what other advantages belong to the Jewish people if automatic salvation is not one of them. By his very question, Paul shows that he thought that these Jewish people who had not trusted in Jesus were still ethnically Jewish, even as did Jeremiah (cf. Jer. 9:26 above). The point in Romans 2:28–29 is that the remnant, the Jewish followers of Jesus, by having fulfilled the requirements of what constitutes Jewishness—physical descent and spiritual circumcision—are not the only Jews, but in reality they are the truest of all Jews.

Spiritual Israel—Romans 9:6. Those who want to "spiritualize" the word "Israel" and change its meaning often point to Romans 9:6: "But it is not as though the word of God has failed. For they are not all Israel who are descended from Israel." Although some maintain that in this verse God has expanded Israel into a spiritual Israel, consisting of both Jewish and Gentile believers, that is not at all what Paul meant. Rather, he is speaking of Jewish believers, the remnant, as a sub-group within Israel. Since Jewish believers in Jesus are Abraham's descendants by both physical and spiritual descent, this faithful remnant is the true Israel.

The context supports a reference here to Jewish believers. Paul began this major section of Romans (chapters 9–11) by expressing his heartfelt concern for "my brothers, my own flesh and blood. . . . They are Israelites" (Rom. 9:3–4 HCSB). In this passage, Paul has identified ethnic Jewish people, who have not believed in Jesus as Messiah, as Israelites. Then, in Romans 9:7–13, he expounds on God's sovereign choices for Abraham's descendants. The apostle's main idea in Romans 9:6 is that, although it seems that God's promises have failed when the bulk of Israel did not believe in Jesus, God's Word certainly did not fail. As proof, Paul argues that there is a spiritual Israel, a remnant, even within ethnic Israel.

In addition to the contextual argument, there is a lexical argument for interpreting Romans 9:6–8 as speaking of Jewish believers in Jesus. Arnold Fruchtenbaum has done an extensive word study, reviewing each of the seventy-three uses of "Israel" in the New Testament. In each case, it refers to the physical descendants of Abraham, Isaac, and Jacob.[3] Only Romans 9:6 and one other possible text (Gal. 6:16, see below) have been proposed as exceptions to this rule. But it seems unlikely that Paul would use the word in such an unusual way, particularly because interpreting this passage as speaking of Jewish followers of Jesus fits the context far better.

So, in Romans 9:6, Paul has characterized messianic Jews as the true Israel by virtue of both their physical descent and their faith in the Messiah Jesus. According to Paul, God keeps His promises to the Jewish people through the true Israel, the Jewish followers of Messiah Jesus. Paul is not saying the church is the true Israel; rather he is arguing that the truest of all Israel are the Jewish believers in Jesus who are both ethnically part of Israel and, as the remnant, spiritually faithful to the God of Israel.

The Israel of God—Galatians 6:16. One common verse used to maintain that Israel and the church are now one is Galatians 6:16: "And those who will walk by this rule, peace and mercy be upon them, and upon the Israel of God." The phrase "the Israel of God" has been a source of great contention, with the majority of evangelical Christian interpreters taking the expression to refer to the church universal as the true Israel. However, for several reasons a more likely interpretation is that Paul began by blessing all who followed his teaching and then added a special blessing for ethnic Jewish believers in Jesus (the Israel of God).

First, taking this as a special blessing for Jewish followers of Jesus fits the normal syntax of the Greek conjunction *and* as a continuative or conjunctive usage. Paul would be blessing those "who walk by this rule *and* the Israel of God." This is the most simple and common way to understand the conjunction. To see this as referring to the church would require an unusual usage, translating the word with an explicative usage ("even"). Then the translation would be a blessing upon those "who walk by rule, even the Israel of God." As noted New Testament scholar S. Lewis Johnson correctly states, "We should avoid the rarer grammatical usages when the common ones make good sense."[4]

A second argument is based on the usage of the word "Israel." Of the seventy-three usages, this would be the only one that does not refer to physical descendants of Abraham, Isaac, and Jacob (see above).[5] It is unlikely that Paul decided to use the word in a "spiritual" sense when every other time he used it as literally referring to the people of Israel.

Third, understanding the "Israel of God" to refer to the faithful Jewish remnant conforms to the context far better. At the end of the epistle, having rebuked those who were demanding circumcision in addition to faith as a requirement for justification before God, Paul certainly wanted to bless everyone in Galatia who supported his teaching. However, some might have viewed Paul's sharp rebuke as attacking all Jewish believers. Therefore, Paul added a specific, additional blessing for the Jewish believers who agreed with him. They were "the Israel of God," the loyal Jewish remnant of Israel.

Jewish Spiritual Leadership—Matthew 21:33–46. The parable of the landowner is a passage that is often used to allege that God has replaced Israel with the church. This text is not used with the softened terminology of fulfillment or expansion theology but rather with a blunt assertion of supersessionism. In the parable told by the Lord Jesus, the vine-growers would not receive the servants of the vineyard owner and they ultimately killed his son. Therefore, the listeners proclaimed that the vineyard owner should rent out the vineyard to other vine-growers (Matt. 21:41). After telling the story, the Lord pointed to Psalm 118:22, a messianic prediction foretelling the Messiah's rejection by the "builders," or the spiritual leaders of Israel (Matt. 21:42). He concludes, "Therefore, I say to you, the kingdom of God will be taken away from you and given to a people, producing the fruit of it" (Matt. 21:43). But does this text actually teach that God would replace Israel with the church?

As the surrounding verses indicate, the answer is no. The parable is not about the Gentile church replacing Israel but rather about a change in the leadership of Israel. This interpretation is supported by the words that immediately follow the parable and the Lord's citation of Psalm 118. The text identifies the response of first-century Jewish leaders to the teaching of Jesus, saying, "When the chief priests and the Pharisees heard His parables, they understood that He was speaking about them" (Matt 21:45). The Messiah Jesus is not speaking of Gentile Christians replacing Israel but about the faithful remnant of Israel, the Jewish followers of Jesus, replacing the priests and Pharisees as the spiritual leadership of Israel. The remnant's faithfulness to God made them the true spiritual leaders of the Jewish people. They might even be rejected, just as Jesus had been rejected, but as the remnant, they now functioned as Israel's true spiritual leaders.

Some have objected that Jesus' words foretold an ethnic change, saying the kingdom will be given to a "people" (or nation, *ethnos* in Greek) producing the fruit of the kingdom. Yet, New

Testament scholar David L. Turner has shown that by the first century, the word *ethnos* was already being used for social groups *within* a particular nation and that the singular word for "nation" was frequently used in the Hebrew Bible of the nation of Israel. He concludes that the word "'nation' is not used here of an ethnic entity but an ethical one, indicating that the Jerusalem religious establishment would be replaced as Israel's leaders by the Messianic remnant, whose leaders will . . . lead Israel in bearing the fruit of righteousness to God."[6]

One New Man—Ephesians 2:11–22. Some have asserted that Ephesians 2:11–22 teaches that God overcame the enmity between Jews and Gentiles by uniting both groups in Israel. But this passage is in reality the most foundational about the unification of Jews and Gentiles in the universal church, not Israel. At the outset of this text, Paul identifies *alienation* as the essential problem that existed between Jews and Gentiles (2:11–12). This estrangement is rooted in the contrast between Israel who were the people of God by covenant, and the Gentiles or pagans, who had no covenant promises, no messianic hope, and who were "without God in the world" (v. 12). One specific aspect of the dire situation of Gentiles was that they were "excluded from the citizenship of Israel" (v. 12 HCSB).

God resolved the separation between Jews and Gentiles by providing *reconciliation* for them through the Messiah Jesus (2:13–19). In a summary statement, Paul uses a contrast ("but now"; v. 13) to remind Gentiles who were formerly far off that they have been brought near to God and to the Jewish people by the Messiah Jesus' atoning death (vv. 13–15). As a result of that atonement, God made "the two" (Jews and Gentiles who believe) into "one new man" (v. 15), reconciled "them both in one body" (v. 16; the church), and made them both "fellow citizens with the saints" (v. 19).

Having described the problem of alienation and explained God's solution as reconciliation, Paul presents the result of Messiah's work: *unification*. The unified body of the Messiah Jesus is pictured as a spiritual temple. In this metaphor of a temple, the Messiah is the chief cornerstone, holding it all together. The apostles and prophets form the foundation, upon which the building is constructed, and individual believers, Jews and Gentiles alike, are the building blocks cemented together by the Spirit of God (2:20–22).

Some have maintained that Paul's point in Ephesians 2:11–22 was that God reconciled believing Jews and Gentiles by joining the Gentiles to Israel. The basis of this idea is that in verse 12, Paul says Gentiles were previously "excluded from the citizenship of Israel" (HCSB) and in verse 19, through the Messiah Jesus, Gentiles are now "fellow citizens with the saints."

However, that last phrase is not saying that Gentiles and Jews had been united as citizens of Israel. Rather, God united them in a completely new entity, the church. First, Paul says that God's solution to the alienation of Jews and Gentiles was to make them into "one new man" (v. 15). The word "new" (*kainos*) refers to something that is new in nature or kind; it did not exist before.[7] When people speak of getting a *new* car, they generally mean obtaining a vehicle they did not previously own. That is not this word "*new*." The word *kainos* would be more like someone declaring they had just invented something entirely new: "a horseless carriage." The "one new man" does not refer to Israel but to something completely new, the church that began at Pentecost (Acts 2).

Second, this one new man, pictured as a temple, is built upon "the foundation of the apostles and prophets" (Eph. 2:20). Therefore, this new community does not join Gentile believers to Israel but instead joins Jewish and Gentile followers of Jesus together in an entirely new community, the church. Moreover, the prophets mentioned are not Old Testament prophets but New Testament ones. This is evident in Ephesians 3:4–6, where it states that the secret of the church, where Jews and Gentiles have been united spiritually, was not known in previous generations but "it has **now** been revealed to His holy apostles and prophets" (v. 5). This clearly identifies them as New Testament apostles and prophets.

Therefore, Gentile alienation was overcome not by adding Gentile Christians into Israel but by forming an entirely new entity, the church, which is the body of the Messiah Jesus. Jews and Gentiles who have faith in Jesus are now "fellow citizens" with all followers of Jesus ("the saints") in this body. Paul goes on to say that this entity, the church, was unknown in ages past (Eph. 3:5), and that its unique feature is the full spiritual equality of Jews and Gentiles (Eph. 3:6).

A second misunderstanding of this passage is to view it as teaching that Jewish believers in Messiah Jesus have lost their distinct national identity as Jews. Plainly, Paul has not affirmed that Jews and Gentiles have lost their ethnic identities. For example, he continues to call Gentile believers "Gentiles" (Rom. 11:13) and calls upon them to show their appreciation for their Jewish believing brethren (Rom. 15:26–27). Paul identified himself as Jewish and a follower of the Messiah Jesus (Acts 21:39; Rom. 11:1, 13–14). For this reason, John Stott, commenting on Ephesians 2:15, writes, "Not that the facts of human differentiation are removed. Men remain men and women, women; Jews remain Jews and Gentiles, Gentiles. But inequality before God is abolished. There is a new unity in Christ."[8]

One more question we should ask is, what overlap, if any, is there between Israel and the church? The answer is that Jewish followers of Jesus are related to both of these distinct communities. As part of ethnic Israel, messianic Jews are the faithful remnant of Israel, even as Romans 11:1–5 describes them. Just as there were seven thousand in Israel, a faithful remnant who did not bow "the knee to Baal" in Elijah's day, although the rest of the nation had strayed from faithfulness to the God of Israel, so "there has also come to be at the present time a remnant according to God's gracious choice" (v. 5). This is the faithful remnant of Jewish people who believe in the Jewish Messiah Yeshua (Jesus) although vast majority of Jewish people do not yet believe in Him.

While maintaining ethnic distinctions, just as Ephesians 2:11–22 states, Jewish and Gentile believers have been united in the body of the Messiah—Jewish believers being the Jewish wing of the church and Gentile Christians, the Gentile wing. The way to visualize the overlapping role of Jewish believers is with this diagram:

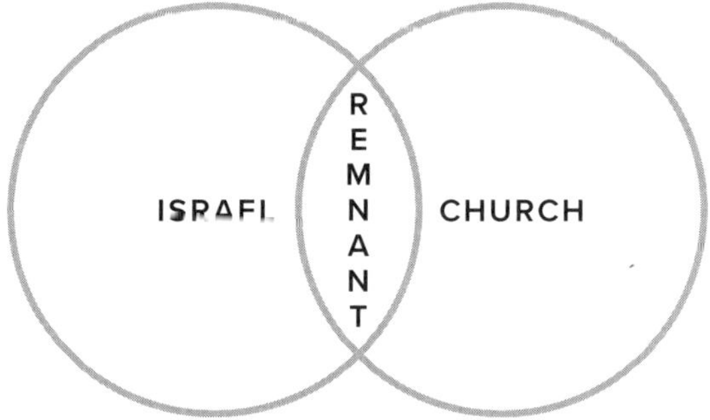

This Venn diagram shows how messianic Jewish believers, are both the remnant of Israel and the Jewish wing of the church at the very same time.

The church and Israel are clearly distinct. They each began at different times and are composed of different people: Israel has an ethnic composition (physical descendants of Abraham, Isaac, and Jacob) while the church has a spiritual composition (all those who have trusted in Jesus the Messiah in this age, both Jews and Gentiles). Yet, both Israel and the church are, in some sense, chosen peoples. How that can be without their being one and the same will be addressed next.

DIFFERENT ELECTIONS

God's choice of Israel has resulted in that nation being called "the chosen people" (cf. Deut. 7:6–7; Rom. 11:28). Similarly, God has also chosen individual believers to become members of the church as revealed in Ephesians 1:4, "He chose us in Him." As a result, some have concluded that the election of the church has resulted in it becoming part of Israel. However, the passages in the New Testament that affirm both the choice of Israel and the choice of the church indicate that they are chosen in different ways.

Israel's National Election

Israel's election is national, referring to God's choice of Israel as a distinct ethnic people (Deut. 14:2). Even though most Jewish people still do not believe in Jesus the Messiah, God's choice of Israel to be His ethnic people in Jesus the Messiah remains true. The New Testament evidence for the continued election of Israel despite unbelief in Jesus is Romans 11:28–29. There, Paul begins by saying that "from the standpoint of the gospel they are enemies for your sake" (Rom. 11:28a), expressing Israel's opposition to the message of Jesus the Messiah. This is advantageous to Gentile believers, as Paul noted previously in Romans 11:11, because of the Jewish rejection of the gospel, "salvation has come to the Gentiles."

Yet, despite the majority of the Jewish people being opposed to the gospel, "from the standpoint of God's choice they are beloved for the sake of the fathers" (Rom. 11:28b). This shows that God views Israel, despite unbelief, as elect or chosen, and as such they remain beloved. The word "loved" in Scripture is frequently associated with choice. For example, the Scriptures say, "I have loved (chosen) Jacob; but I have hated (rejected) Esau" (Mal. 1:2–3; Rom. 9:13). The point Paul makes is that Jewish opposition to the gospel in no way negates God's national election of Israel for "His great name" (1 Sam. 12:22; cf. Deut. 7:6–9; 14:2). The reason is that "God's gracious gifts and calling are irrevocable" (Rom. 11:29 HCSB).

The Church's Spiritual Election

The church has a different kind of election, one that crosses national boundaries and is distinctly spiritual—it is an election to salvation. In Ephesians 1:4, speaking of individual members of the church, Paul says God "chose us in Him before the foundation of the world, that we would be holy and blameless before Him." This choice is linked to God's loving predestination to adoption (Eph. 1:5) and redemption through the sacrificial death of Messiah Jesus (Eph.1:7). Members of the church are indeed elect, but God's choice pertains to their forgiveness of sins and not their ethnicity.

Clearly, Israel and the church are both chosen but in completely different ways. Even so, some have argued that followers of Jesus are called Abraham's seed (descendants; Gal. 3:29). Does that not indicate that the church and Israel are one and the same? It is to this issue we now turn.

DIFFERENT RELATIONSHIP TO ABRAHAM

The verse that is likely used most often to maintain that the New Testament changes the identification of the covenant people of God from the Jewish people to the church is Galatians 3:16. It states, "Now the promises were spoken to Abraham and to his seed. He does not say, 'And to seeds,' as referring to many but rather to one, 'And to your seed,' that is, Christ." Those who cite this verse acknowledge that in the Old Testament, the Jewish people were clearly the recipients of the promises of the Abrahamic covenant. However, they also assert that Galatians 3:16 changes the beneficiary of the covenantal promises to Jesus Christ alone. Additionally, they develop their argument by citing Galatians 3:29: "And if you belong to Christ, then you are Abraham's descendants (seed), heirs according to the promise." Since believers today are in Christ, it is alleged they (not the Jewish people) are the true seed of Abraham and therefore the true recipients of all the Abrahamic promises rather than the Jewish people. Based on this, they affirm that in the New Testament, the Jewish people are no longer considered the seed of Abraham.

Yet Paul, when writing about Israel and the Jewish people, says of himself, "I too am an Israelite, a descendant of Abraham" (Rom. 11:1), He recognized that the Israelites (Jewish people) remain the physical descendants of Abraham. Paul also maintained that the covenants belong to ethnic Israel and that God's gifts to the Jewish people are irrevocable (Rom. 9:4–5; 11:28–29). Paul would not contradict himself, so he must have meant something else in Galatians 3. Actually, Paul's message in Galatians is not changing the meaning of the Old Testament, but rather he was highlighting a promise already found in the Abrahamic covenant. We need to go back to Genesis to grasp Paul's message in Galatians 3.

To begin to understand Paul, we need to understand that the Hebrew word for "seed" is never plural in form. Sometimes it is used collectively for a whole group and sometimes it is used individually, referring to a specific person. The best English equivalent is "offspring" which can be used to refer to many descendants (a collective sense) and to one descendant (an individual sense). So, in Galatians 3:16, when Paul wrote, not "as referring to many but rather to one," he is referring to an individual use of the word "seed."

Paul's discussion about the seed is taken from Genesis 22:17–18.[9] These two verses use the word "seed" three times. The first use has the collective sense: "I will greatly bless you, and I will greatly multiply your seed" (v. 17a), clearly referring to the whole Jewish people who would descend from Abraham. The second usage of seed refers to an individual: Abraham's "seed shall possess the gate of their [literally "**his**"] enemies. In your seed all the nations of the earth shall be blessed" (vv. 17b–18). It is this second seed who will rule over His enemies and bless the whole world. The evidence that this second use of seed is referring to an individual is that the pronoun referring back to that seed is singular (lit. the seed "shall possess the gate of *his* enemies").

How can the text switch from a collective sense in its first use to an individual one in its second? The Hebrew grammar of the verb in the middle of v. 17, "And he shall possess," explains this change. It is not the typical Hebrew consecutive sense but rather begins a new sentence with a new thought. Therefore, the promises in Genesis 22:17–18 are two-fold. First, Abraham's collective seed, the Jewish people, will multiply greatly (22:17a). Second, Abraham's individual seed, the future Messiah, will rule over His enemies (22:17b) and bless the whole world (22:18).[10] With this as background, we can finally understand Galatians 3.

Paul's argument in Galatians as a whole is that Gentiles need not convert to Judaism before believing in Jesus, the Jewish Messiah. So he declared, "The Scripture, foreseeing that God would justify the Gentiles by faith, preached the gospel beforehand to Abraham, saying, 'All the nations will be blessed in you'" (Gal. 3:8, quoting Gen. 12:3). Part of the Abrahamic covenant was the anticipation of blessing the Gentiles as Gentiles.

Then, in Galatians 3:16, citing Genesis 22:18, Paul emphasized that he was not discussing the collective seed but rather that the source of Gentile blessing would derive from the individual messianic seed: "Now the promises were spoken to Abraham and to his seed. He does not say, 'And to seeds,' as referring to many but rather to one, 'And to your seed,' that is, Christ." Therefore, if Gentiles believe in the Messiah Jesus, they need not convert to Judaism first because, if they "belong to Christ, then [they] are Abraham's descendants, heirs according to the promise" (Gal. 3:29). If they are in Christ, then they are already spiritual descendants of Abraham and heirs of the spiritual promises (Gal. 3:29) of the Abrahamic covenant just as the Scriptures in Genesis foretold. Galatians 3 does not change the meaning of the Abrahamic covenant or the beneficiaries. Rather, it highlights what God had promised the Gentiles all the way back in Genesis. They would be related to Abraham by spiritual descent through their faith in the Messiah. At the same time, Jewish people would remain the physical offspring of Abraham through their descent from Isaac and Jacob.

CONCLUSION

The church's historical tradition of identity theft of God's promises to ethnic Israel leads to much of the confusion believers feel when the State of Israel or the Jewish people are in the news. When there is a conflict in the Middle East or a surge of antisemitism around the world, Christians will often see these situations as irrelevant to them because they consider themselves the true Israel and the real chosen people. But, according to Scripture, Israel and the church are distinct entities. As such, they have different beginnings, are composed of different people, experience a different category of election and are related to Abraham in different ways. There is no basis for blending these two entities into one. And furthermore, it's at these times that Gentile Christians must heed Paul's warning not to become "arrogant" toward Jewish people (Rom. 11:18) nor to be ignorant that God has a glorious plan for the people of Israel (Rom. 11:25–27).

Chapter Four

WHY CHRISTIANS SHOULD CARE ABOUT ISRAEL AND THE JEWISH PEOPLE

"I just don't care about Israel . . . that much."

This was said by a prominent Christian conservative political commentator during an interview with a journalist. He elaborated, "I'm not just America first. I'm an American chauvinist. I only care about my own country." He went on to say that Israel was just like any other country to him and a small one at that. He stated there was nothing special or significant about Israel, or the Jewish people for that matter, and therefore was utterly unconcerned about Israel.

Historically, American Christians have been some of the strongest supporters of Israel and among the greatest advocates for the Jewish people. But in recent years some, like this commentator, are increasingly adopting a callous indifference, or worse, a hostile attitude.

As you know from the previous chapters of this book, I have a profound disagreement with this perspective. I am convinced the Scriptures teach that we must be concerned about Israel and the Jewish people. To tie the themes of this book together, here are four biblical reasons all followers of Jesus should care about Israel, both the people and the state.

1. Israel is distinct among the nations.

The first reason to care is because Israel has a distinctive status among all the peoples and nations of the world. It has always been a serious mistake to consider Israel to be "just another country" or "just another people." And it is not because of any Jewish accomplishments or superiority. Israel's distinctiveness is rooted in God's sovereign choice of this people. Moses made this clear when he wrote,

> "The Lord your God has chosen you to be a people for His own possession out of all the peoples who are on the face of the earth. The Lord did not set His love on you nor choose you because you were more in number than any of the peoples, for you were the fewest of all peoples, but because the Lord loved you and kept the oath which He swore to your forefathers." (Deut. 7:6–8)

Plainly, Israel's distinctiveness is a result of God's sovereign election.

One of the most common slurs I have personally heard against Jewish people is that they act superior or consider themselves more important than others because of God's choice. Frankly, most Jewish people, when pushed, lament being the "chosen people" because of its related persecution. It is not unusual for Jewish people to joke about asking God if He would mind choosing some other people for a change.

Despite God's choice of Israel, in the sixth century BC, Moab treated Israel as just another nation. They celebrated the Babylonian invasion of Judah, reflecting Moab's longtime hostility to Israel, going back nearly a millennium, when Balak, king of Moab, attempted to hire Balaam to curse Israel (Num. 22:5–6). The Moabite glee at Babylon's destruction caused the prophet Ezekiel to proclaim judgment. Moab had declared, "Behold, the house of Judah is like all the nations" (Ezek. 25:8). They failed to see that God's choice made Israel a distinctive nation. Their serious error of judgment is the same one being made today. Israel is not like any other nation. The Jewish people have unconditional and eternal covenants with God. The Lord promised that the Moabite perspective would cause Him to "execute judgments on Moab" (Ezek. 25:11). We must learn this lesson from Moab's failure. Israel is distinct among the nations because of God's choice and He expects us to recognize and care for His chosen people.

2. God loves the Jewish people forever.

A second reason to care about Israel today is because God has an eternal love for the Jewish people. Through the prophet Jeremiah, the Lord announced to Israel, "I have loved you with an everlasting love; therefore I have drawn you with lovingkindness" (Jer. 31:3). Now this declaration of love came after many years and many occasions of Israel being rebellious. Yet, God reaffirmed His commitment to His people. This is a terrific example of grace. God loves Israel not because the nation earned it but because God bestowed His undeserved kindness on His people.

As we have seen in previous chapters, some may object that when Israel rejected Jesus as the Messiah, God rejected Israel and gave His promises and His love over to the church. But not the apostle Paul. He maintained that "God has not rejected His people whom He foreknew" (Rom. 11:2). Furthermore, Paul declared that even though the Jewish people oppose the gospel, "they are beloved for the sake of the fathers" (Rom. 11:28). God's unconditional and everlasting love for Israel is the reason the Lord will restore Israel one day, when they will seek the Messiah Jesus (Hos. 3:4–5) and "all Israel will be saved" (Rom. 11:26).

We need to love whom God loves, cherish whom the Lord cherishes, and care for the people God cares for. The commentator I mentioned at the outset stated that he loves his own family, not anyone else's. In the same way, he said, he loves America, not some other nation. This is a shortsighted and narrow-minded perspective.

Jamie Boskey, a graduate of Moody Bible Institute, had a different viewpoint. Some years ago when a student, she told me that she was going to spend her summer break reading the Bible to discern what broke the heart of the Lord Jesus. In fact, she studied the Scriptures to discern for whom God's great concern and compassion was greatest. In August, she returned to school with tremendous excitement. Jamie told me she now knew what broke the Lord's heart and was determined to focus on that from then on. And what did she discover? Jamie told me that, in the Gospels, the only two times the Lord Jesus wept was over the unbelief of Israel (Luke 19:41–44; John 11:32–45[1]). His great love for His people made their rejection of Him break His heart. Amazingly, here was this student, not Jewish herself, not even a Jewish Studies major, who committed to love the Jewish people and minister to them for the rest of her life. Why? Because she wanted to love whom God loves. Now, more than ten years later that is exactly what she is doing from her home in Israel.

3. God has compassion for Israel.

A third reason we need to care for Israel is because of the Lord's great compassion for His people. God never forgets the sorrow and suffering of the Jewish people. Frankly, it is astounding and troubling how readily people forget the pain and persecution Jewish people have experienced. In my own lifetime, I have observed the steady growth of Holocaust denial. It has become mainstream for some journalists to give a platform to those who deny Hitler's murder of six million Jews or even open their microphones to those who wish Hitler had succeeded in eradicating all the Jewish people. Despite this terrible turn, most of society is uncaring and unconcerned.

Consider what happened after the horrific massacre carried out by Hamas on October 7, 2023—an early morning attack in which terrorists stormed across the border of Israel from Gaza, murdering children and their parents, burning people alive or beheading them, sexually assaulting and then mutilating women, and murdering young people at a music festival. They murdered 1,200 people and took 251 captives to the terror tunnels of Gaza, including infants, toddlers, and aged Holocaust survivors. And immediately, groups in America, especially at universities, blamed Israel and called this justifiable resistance. Others called it a false flag operation and charged the Israel Defense Forces with being the actual perpetrators of the attack. Finally, many condemned Israel for going to war with Hamas to restore national security in the State of Israel.

Holocaust denial and Hamas support are just two examples of circumstances that have caused Israelis and Jewish people around the world to wonder if anyone has compassion for the suffering of the Jewish people. This is not new. Even in ancient times, Israel had the same question, wondering if even the Lord had forgotten them. He replied to His people through the prophet Isaiah:

> But Zion said, "The LORD has forsaken me, and the Lord has forgotten me." "Can a woman forget her nursing child and have no compassion on the son of her womb? Even these may forget, but I will not forget you. Behold, I have inscribed you on the palms of My hands; your walls are continually before Me." (Isa. 49:14–16)

The Lord's promise is clear. His compassion for Israel is even greater than that of a nursing mother for her child. Israel's sufferings and sorrows are ever present in the Lord's mind and heart. He is present with them in all their pain.

Through the years, many of my fellow Jewish people have asked me about the Holocaust, wondering, "Where was God when the six million died?" My answer is always the same, just as it says in Isaiah 63:9, "In all their affliction He was afflicted." God was always with His people, in the ghettos and camps, in the gas chambers and crematoria. The Lord was with His people, suffering with them in their pain. His compassion for their suffering never failed. He was even present with them on that horrific morning of October 7. That is why those who love the God of Israel and follow the Messiah of Israel must share His compassion for the people of Israel. We who reflect the light of the Messiah to this world must also shine His heartfelt compassion for Israel, His "treasured ones" (Ps. 83:3). Our mandate is to fulfill Isaiah 40:1, "'Comfort, O comfort My people,' says your God."

4. We can care for the Messiah Jesus Himself.

Fourth, we should care for Israel because it is a way to show our love for the Messiah Jesus. God's people would certainly want to express their love for the Messiah Jesus Himself in some tangible way. To do that, many will commit to feeding and clothing the poor. They will cite the parable of the sheep and the goats (Matt. 25:31–46), and its call to care for the needy as in the King's statement, "'Truly I say to you, to the extent that you did it to one of these brothers of Mine, even the least of them, you did it to Me" (v. 40). People see these verses as evidence that by providing for the poor and homeless, they are caring for the Lord Jesus Himself. Although this is a meaningful and valid application of the parable, it is not closely drawn from its original meaning.

The primary application of this parable is to the Jewish people. Here is why: To begin, the parable is concerned with the end of days judgment of the Gentile nations. The opening paragraph clarifies the time of this judgment ("when the Son of man comes in His glory;" Matt. 25:31) and identifies those being judged ("All the nations will be gathered before Him"; Matt. 25:32). This judgment will take place in the Kidron Valley at the close of the future tribulation period (Zech. 14:3; Joel 3:1–3, 12).

The King will invite those judged as "sheep" to enter the messianic kingdom because they had fed and clothed Him, invited Him in as a stranger and visited Him in prison (Matt. 25:35–36). The righteous among the nations will wonder how this was possible and ask:

> "Lord, when did we see You hungry, and feed You, or thirsty, and give You something to drink? And when did we see You a stranger, and invite You in, or naked, and clothe You? When did we see You sick, or in prison, and come to You?" The King will answer and say to them, "Truly I say to you, to the extent that you did it to one of ***these brothers of Mine, even the least of them***, you did it to Me." (vv. 37–40)

This judgment will take place at the end of the tribulation, a period which Jeremiah called "the time of Jacob's distress" (Jer. 30:7), when the Jewish people will be objects of terrible persecution (Rev. 12:13; Matt. 24:21–22). The Lord's words of commendation describe how believers in the tribulation will live out their faith. Their trust in Jesus the Messiah will cause them to express their genuine faith by acting as righteous Gentiles, caring for the physical brothers ("these brothers of Mine") of the Messiah Jesus, the Jewish people.

So how do we apply this today? Of course, caring for any poor and oppressed people is a valid application because of the incarnation—the Lord Jesus is physically related to all humanity. But the primary application is really about how followers of Jesus treat Jewish people today as they increasingly are becoming objects of hatred. The Lord was referring specifically to Jewish people when He called them "these brothers of Mine." In a sense, when we take our stand with the Jewish people, oppose antisemitism and the hatred of the Jewish state, we are not just doing the right thing: We are caring for the Lord Jesus Himself.

CONCLUSION

Some followers of Jesus may think that they do not wish harm to the Jewish people or to Israel but neither do they care if bad things happen to Jews. They may think, "They are not my people, so they do not matter to me." Indifference to the plight of Israel and the Jewish people is just another form of rejecting God's heart for His people. Someone once wrote, "How odd of God to choose the Jews." Ogden Nash is said to have written this reply, "How odd of God to choose the Jews? But not so odd as those who choose the Jewish God but spurn the Jews."

Our faith is built on Jewish promises. We read the Jewish Scriptures. Our eternal redemption was purchased by the Messiah of Israel. We are committed to the God of Israel. With this spiritual inheritance, we dare not reject whom God has chosen or adopt indifference toward those for whom the Lord is passionate. We who love the God of Israel and follow the Messiah of Israel must not be uncaring to the people of Israel. He calls us to love His people Israel as an expression of our love for the Messiah Jesus Himself.

Chapter Five

BLESSING ISRAEL: WHAT'S IN IT FOR ME?

Someone once told me to remember that everyone is listening to their favorite radio station, WIIFM—those call letters stand for ***What's In It For Me***?

It is human nature to seek our own personal benefit when asked to change our perspective or behavior. This leads to the question, if I am asked to feel concern for Israel and the Jewish people and to act on that care, does the Bible promise me any benefit? The answer is yes. Of course, there is always the profit of doing what is right, but there also are some practical benefits for thinking and acting rightly about the Jewish people. As the takeaway of this book, here are three positive outcomes for caring about Israel.

SPIRITUAL SECURITY

So often in my classes, when teaching about God's faithfulness to Israel and the distinct natures of Israel and the church, some student would ask, "Does this really matter at all?" They would be surprised when my answer always took them back to the argument of the book of Romans. At the end of chapter 8, Paul declares that nothing will ever separate us from the love of God in the Messiah Jesus:

> For I am convinced that neither death, nor life, nor angels, nor principalities, nor things present, nor things to come, nor powers, nor height, nor depth, nor any other created thing, will be able to separate us from the love of God, which is in Christ Jesus our Lord. (Rom. 8:38–39)

With that statement, Paul launches his section on God's concern for and faithfulness to Israel (Rom. 9–11). I have seen books and commentaries state that this section on Israel was a digression from Paul's argument—a Pauline tangent. Nothing could be further from the truth.

The reality is that throughout the book of Romans there is an unseen objector, questioning everything Paul has written. At each juncture, Paul anticipates the objection and then answers it. The doubt of this unseen objector could be expressed like this: "What do you mean nothing will separate from God's love? The Jewish people were beloved by God at one time. But they failed to believe in the Messiah Jesus so God wrote them off. He will do the same to us if we are not perfectly faithful." Paul responds by vindicating God, showing His faithfulness to Israel and so proving He will be faithful to us as well. In a sense, Israel becomes the ultimate object lesson and guarantee of God's faithfulness.

So, one of the great benefits we can derive from understanding God's faithfulness to Israel is the sure knowledge that we are secure in God's love. Just as God will keep His promises to the Jewish people, He will keep every promise to us. We can be spiritually secure, not looking over our shoulders constantly, on every bad day, wondering if we are in or out. We serve a Lord who is faithful and true to all His promises.

PERSONAL PEACE

A second benefit for seeking the good of Israel is personal peace. This is derived from Psalm 122:6, "Pray for the peace of Jerusalem: 'May they prosper who love you.'" To break this verse down, the peace we are to pray for is not just the absence of conflict. The word *shalom* ("peace") implies wholeness, completeness, and well-being. Of course, praying for the complete well-being of Israel would include praying that Jewish people would come to know Yeshua (Jesus), the Prince of Peace, as their true Redeemer (Rom. 10:1).

Also, when praying for Jerusalem, we are not interceding just for the city, but since it is the capital of Israel, we are praying for the well-being of *all* the people of Israel. And the result, for those who love Jerusalem enough to pray, would be that they will "prosper." Although this word *shalah* ("prosper") can mean material prosperity, it also can refer to rest, ease, or inner peace. For example, it is used in Job 3:26, "I have no *peace*, no quietness; I have no rest, but only turmoil" (NIV), referring to personal peace or emotional stability.

It is unlikely that praying for the well-being of Israel means doing so can bring material prosperity. Rather, this verse is saying that a benefit we can obtain by praying for Israel's wholeness is personal peace and emotional stability. How does this work? I am not sure anyone can know for certain. Perhaps peace and stability come from knowing we are praying in obedience to God's Word. Or it may just be that it is a kindness the Lord grants when we pray according to His heart for His people Israel. Regardless, it is a good outcome when we pray for the peace of Jerusalem.

INDIVIDUAL BLESSING

The first chapter of this book began with a discussion of a US Senator affirming his belief that as a nation, we are to bless Israel in order to be blessed as a nation. Although he could not identify which verse taught this, Genesis 12:3 does say, "And I will bless those who bless you, and the one who curses you I will curse." It appears that this is a truism for nations across history. When I was a student at Moody Bible Institute, Dr. George Sweeting, then president of the Institute, wrote an open letter to President-Elect Jimmy Carter, encouraging him in this area. Dr. Sweeting stated that the United States was always a safe haven for Jewish people and a strong supporter of the State of Israel. He identified these policies as an actual source of God's blessing on our nation and encouraged the new president to continue to bless Israel and the Jewish people. Obviously, the Genesis 12:3 principle applies to nations, but what about individuals?

When discussing whether this principle applied to individuals, my colleague and more importantly, my good friend Dr. Michael Vanlaningham, offered to write his perspective on the question of personal blessing. So, I will give Mike the last word, not just for this section but for the lesson of this whole book.

✡ ✡ ✡ ✡ ✡

> The Lord said to Abram, "I will bless those who bless you . . ." (Gen. 12:3). I believe this ancient promise is still in play. While much of the discussion of the Abrahamic Covenant circles around how nations treat Israel, I'm convinced there is also a more individualized application of it. Historically, the nations that have been most welcoming to the Jewish people have prospered, and those which have been antagonistic face significant deprivation. God also showers His favor upon *individuals* who seek the welfare of the nation Israel as well as individual Jews. I'll use myself as "Exhibit A" on this point.

God has poured out enormous blessings on me, my wife, Sue, and our family. This is all of grace. But I also wonder if part of the kindness of God to us has been because of His faithfulness to the Genesis 12 covenant. Throughout my long academic career, I have preferred to focus on teaching and therefore, published relatively few articles. But what I have published has defended the prominence of Israel in God's redemptive program. I've taught the book of Romans over fifty times, always emphasizing the critical part Israel plays in salvation history as we waded through Romans 9–11. We have given to various ministries designed to take the gospel to the Jewish people. I have led about thirty tours to Israel so that the believers who join us can see for themselves God's powerful work on behalf of the Jewish people. It has been my pleasure to partner with my messianic Jewish colleagues in many ministry opportunities.

In spite of a life career in various ministries not known as typically wealth-producing, we have retired more securely than we ever thought possible. More than financial security, our grown children, their spouses, and our older grandchildren have trusted Jesus as their Savior and are neck deep in serving in their respective churches. This is the richest endowment of all. My experience has convinced me that believers must seek the promised blessing and heed the warning of Genesis 12, by pursuing the welfare of the offspring of Abraham, Isaac, and Jacob.

Afterword

When professing Christians post vile, hate filled anti-Jewish messages on social media, it gets my attention. Moody Publishers has marketed this book extensively on social media. There have been many positive responses and the book has been well received. Yet what has been most startling is that so many professed followers of the Lord Jesus, despite not having read the book, have reacted on social media with posts expressing virulent hatred of the Jewish people and the State of Israel.

The comments are shocking and frankly despicable, comparable to Nazi propaganda. Some quote Bible verses out of context to describe Jewish people and Israel as permanently rejected by God while others misuse Scripture to identify all Jewish people as uniquely satanic. Others charge blood libels, repeat anti-Jewish tropes, or defame Judaism and Jewish people.

Since so many have written ghastly comments about Jewish people, Moody Publishers has graciously allowed me to add this afterword. I'll try to summarize some of the most common expressions of Jew hatred evident in those social media comments and to counter them briefly. It would take another whole book to address all of them, but this short response must suffice for now.

ANGRY REPLACEMENT THEOLOGY

Replacement theology, an ancient teaching of the church, need not be intrinsically hateful of Jewish people. In fact, there are many respectable and responsible Bible interpreters who hold that church has replaced the Jewish people as the true Israel. What I am referring to by *angry replacement theology* is a new form, often embraced by social media posters, who tie this view to a vitriolic hatred of the Jewish people.

Replacement theology has been a problem since the first century. Some have called this teaching "supersessionism." Likely, Paul was responding to an incipient, supersessionist perspective when he wrote Romans 9–11 to correct it. This scriptural rebuke fell on deaf ears. In the second century, Justin Martyr was the first church father to express replacement theology explicitly. By the time John Chrysostom wrote his *Homilies Against the Jews* in the fourth century, supersessionism had evolved into the basis for virulent Jew hatred by the church and remained so until the Holocaust. After the Nazi genocide, the church tended to move away from this erroneous teaching. In recent decades, however, there has been a growing return to supersessionism, although not necessarily holding an anti-Jewish attitude. However, in recent years, some Christians have morphed their supersessionism into an angry, political form of replacement theology, embracing Jew hatred as an outgrowth of it.

Out of Context Verses

One of the ways angry replacement theology is expressed on social media is by its adherents quoting out of context, allegedly supersessionist, biblical verses. Just by writing the verse, they think that their citation is the end of the discussion. They make no attempt to read these passages in context or to harmonize them with other biblical texts that affirm God's continuing love and concern for Jewish people. If any other commenter refers to verses about God's faithfulness to the Jewish people, they respond with a vile tirade about the evil of the Jewish people and the anathematizing of any understanding of the Bible that is not supersessionist.

The Synagogue of Satan

Another common idea that angry supersessionists raise on social media is that Jewish people are uniquely satanic. One social media commenter posted, "The book should say: 'How to praise and help satanists.' I'm a Christian and I'm positive that this book is evil and totally against the Bible!" Another wrote, "Just listen to what Jesus thought of the Jewish people—He called them the synagogue of Satan" (Rev. 2:9; 3:9). Where does this idea lead? In the early morning hours of Saturday, January 10, 2026, an arsonist set ablaze a historic synagogue in Jackson, MS. When the suspect, a nineteen-year-old noted for posting Bible verses and identifying as a Christian on social media, was arrested, he explained that he acted against "the synagogue of Satan." At his arraignment, when the judge asked if he understood his constitutional right to an attorney, he replied, "Yes sir, Jesus Christ is Lord."[1]

But does the Lord Jesus characterize all Jewish people as uniquely satanic or the synagogue of Satan? To begin, according to the New Testament, Satan's influence is not limited to the Jewish people but extends to all lost humanity. The apostle John declared that "the whole world lies in the power of the evil one" (1 John 5:19). Paul wrote that Satan, "the god of this world has blinded the minds of the unbelieving so that they might not see the light of the gospel of the glory of Christ" (2 Cor 4:4). Since God loves the whole lost world (John 3:16), it would be wrong to use these other verses to justify believers hating all lost people. In the same way, it's incorrect to use phrases like "the synagogue of Satan" to justify hatred of Jewish people.

Additionally, the Lord Jesus inaugurated His public ministry by going to His hometown synagogue of Nazareth and reading the Scriptures there (Luke 4:14–21). Moreover, Matthew records that the Lord Jesus "went through all the towns and villages, teaching in their synagogues, proclaiming the good news of the kingdom and healing every disease" (Matt. 9:35 NIV). It is utterly unthinkable that the Lord Jesus would have had such positive ministry experiences in a satanic institution.

After the Lord's crucifixion, resurrection, and ascension, the apostle Paul, in his travels, always began his proclamation in synagogues. When he visited the synagogue in Berea, the Jewish people there were described as "noble-minded" (NASB) because they received Paul's message "and examined the Scriptures every day to see if what Paul said was true" (Acts 17:11 NIV). Clearly, Paul's ministry also shows that all synagogues should not be equated with Satan.

So, to whom does the phrase "synagogue of Satan" refer? Dr. Charles Feinberg, founding Academic Dean of the Talbot School of Theology, has suggested that it refers to a group of false teachers advocating the Galatian heresy, that Gentiles needed to be circumcised and convert to Judaism as a prerequisite to putting their trust in Jesus.[2] Adding works to justification was clearly false, and circumcision couldn't make someone genuinely Jewish in God's eyes—that only comes by descent from Abraham, Isaac, and Jacob. That's why these Gentile false teachers are described as "those who say they are Jews and are not" (Rev. 2:9; see also 3:9). The phrase "synagogue of Satan" doesn't even refer to Jewish people but to Gentile legalists who were falsely advocating circumcision as a prerequisite to salvation. It should never be used as a justification for hatred of Jewish people, today or ever.

Not Really the Jewish People

One other way internet trolls express their replacement theology is by denying that Jewish people are really Jewish. They might acknowledge that certain biblical verses do make promises to Israel, but they insist Jewish people today are actually European Gentiles. They base this on an allegation that in the eighth century, the Khazars, a Turkic Ukrainian empire, had converted en masse to Judaism.[3] This claim asserts that Jewish people today are descendants of the Khazars and not connected to the biblical people of Israel, to whom the promises were given.

This theory, so confidently posted as fact on social media, is patently false for three reasons. First, it has been disproved by numerous genetic studies readily available in science journals. Possibly the simplest explanation is from an article in *Science* by Michael Balter, who refers to a 2010 genetic study that found Ashkenazi Jews (allegedly the descendants of the Khazars) "clustered more closely with Middle Eastern and Sephardic Jews, a finding the researchers say is inconsistent with the Khazar hypothesis." Balter concludes "that all three Jewish groups—Middle Eastern, Sephardic, and Ashkenazi—share genome wide genetic markers that distinguish them from other worldwide populations."[4]

Second, the Khazar theory should be rejected based on language. Linguist Alexander Beider has shown that Yiddish, the daily language spoken by Ashkenazi Jews prior to the Holocaust (as opposed to Hebrew, which was a holy language reserved for study and prayer) is primarily Germanic in structure. It contains no Turkic elements, which would be present if the Khazar thesis was true.[5]

Third, the Jewish experience of persecution in medieval Christian Europe kept Jewish people distinctive. European Jews had virtually no social contact with European Gentiles. Moreover, European Christian governments made conversion to Judaism illegal. And even if it were legal, what Gentile would willingly choose to convert to Judaism and become subject to persecution? The discredited Khazar theory of Jewish identity is just one more attempt to deny God's promises to the Jewish people. Overall, whether citing verses out of context, calling Jewish people satanic, or denying their Jewishness altogether, replacement theology is a major source of renewed Christian hatred of Jewish people.

Offended by Jewish Unbelief

Many social media comments reflect outrage that most Jewish people still don't believe in Jesus. They presuppose that the United States is a "Christian nation," and therefore non-Christians should not have the privilege of full citizenship. Moreover, the Jewish State (Israel), because of unbelief, should not be allowed into the community of nations. Their anger at Jewish unbelief is expressed in a variety of ways.

The Talmud

One particular way anger at Jewish unbelief is expressed is by posting memes or making comments about the Jewish

Talmud, particularly referencing what it allegedly says about Jesus, Christians, and Gentiles. They do this without ever having read the Talmud or even knowing what it is. The Talmud is a multi-volume book of Jewish legal arguments, case law, legends, and lore, encompassing 2.5 million words. Less than 1 percent of the Talmud even deals with the issues being cited, and often the comments don't even accurately reflect the Talmud's actual teachings. Most Jewish people and even those who study the Talmud (which is relatively few Jewish people) are utterly unaware of these sections.

Specifically, these commenters express anger that the Talmud allegedly rejects Jesus as a false teacher, who led Israel astray. Many Jewish scholars claim that these few citations aren't really about Jesus of Nazareth. But even if these harsh words in the Talmud are actually about Jesus, they weren't written in a vacuum. The Talmud was codified in the sixth century AD and contained responses to aggressive Christian attacks on the Jewish people. Augustine (AD 354–430), one of the most significant of the church fathers, had developed the "witness theory," arguing that Christians were to persecute Jewish people and force them to wander the earth, even as Cain was cursed to wander. John Chrysostom (AD 347–407), the most noteworthy church father in the eastern church, wrote numerous vile homilies against the Jewish people, including these words: "God always hated the Jews . . . It is incumbent upon all Christians to hate the Jews!" Consequently, it should not be surprising that the Talmud responded with harsh and blasphemous statements about our Messiah. It's similar to Romans 2:24 ("The name of God is blasphemed among the Gentiles because of you"), but in reverse: The words and actions of Christians have caused the name of the Messiah Jesus to be blasphemed among the Jewish people. It is inflammatory to quote these Talmudic phrases, even as the medieval Jew-haters quoted them, while failing to recognize the Christian responsibility in influencing the Jewish sages to make them.

Christ Is King

A common social media response to Jewish unbelief is to simply declare, "Christ is King!" Since followers of Jesus recognize Him as our King, would appear to be a God-honoring statement. However, it has been turned into a triumphalist assertion of domination over the Jewish people. It started when a controversial podcaster began making hateful and conspiratorial comments about Jewish people. Then, the media company for which she worked, founded by an Orthodox Jewish man, fired her. She left, taunting her former colleague, with the words, "Christ is King." Afterwards, other haters of Jews began using this phrase as a taunt against Jewish people. Nick Fuentes, a neo-Nazi white supremacist, held a rally where he called for a "holy war" against the Jews. He declared "we will make them die in the holy war. They will go down, because we have God on our side and they will go down with their satanic master. They have no future in America. The enemies of Christ have no future in this world. Christ is King." The crowd replied to Fuentes' murderous invective by chanting, "Christ is King, Christ is King!"[6]

For nearly twenty years, I have personally signed my letters with the phrase, "All for the King." Obviously, I believe in King Jesus and want to glorify Him. So, how can "Christ is King" be construed as hateful of Jewish people? Jeremy Boreing of *The Daily Wire* gave this explanation:

> How is saying "Christ is King" antisemitic? The same way anything becomes antisemitic—when it is used for the purpose of expressing antisemitism. It's like asking "how does a shovel become a murder weapon?" When it is used to murder someone. This isn't hard. A shovel is not innately a murder weapon. Saying "Christ is King" is not innately antisemitic. It's all about how a thing is used. Saying "Christ is King" for an evil purpose—like using it as a weapon to express your hatred or disdain for the Jews—is a grave sin . . . God will not be mocked. Invoking Him in vain self-promotion, or to troll Jews, or to attack your political rivals is to carry forth His Name in vain.[7]

Clearly, intent matters, and taunting Jewish people who don't believe in Jesus with triumphalist jargon upends gospel proclamation. God has called Jesus followers to change the world by penetration of the gospel message, not domination by it.

Clearly, melding right-wing politics with distorted Christian faith has led to an angry form of Christian nationalism. If Christian faith is essential to being a true American, then any citizen who is not a Christian is suspect. As a result, Christian nationalism makes Jewish people, even politically conservative ones, at best into second class citizens and at worst as enemies of the state.

How different from the Lord Jesus, who wept over Jewish unbelief (Luke 19:41) and longed for Jewish people to follow Him. He anticipated the day when Israel would receive Him as their Messiah (Matt. 23:37–39). The apostle Paul was so heartbroken over Jewish unbelief that he was willing, if it was only possible, to be separated from the Lord Jesus for all eternity, if the Jewish people could be saved (Rom. 9:1–3). His response to Jewish unbelief was not triumphalism or taunting but heartfelt prayer for their salvation (Rom. 10:1).

SPREADING ANTI-JEWISH PROPAGANDA

An accurate way to describe Jew hatred is as a conspiracy theory that attributes all evil in society to the malign influence and actions of the Jewish people. As such, there are many anti-Jewish stereotypes and tropes endlessly repeated on social media. It would take a whole book, not a section in a brief afterward, to respond to them all. I suggest reading Bari Weiss's *How to Fight Anti-Semitism*[8] for a thorough refutation of these lies. Nevertheless, the social media comments made by professing Christians expressing their hatred of Jewish people should be addressed, even if briefly.

Blood Libels

One of the age-old anti-Jewish canards is that Jewish people are innately murderous. In medieval times, Jewish people were falsely accused of poisoning wells causing the bubonic plague and of ritual murder of Christian children, using their blood to make Passover matzohs. The loudest blood libel today is that Israel has committed genocide against Palestinians in the recent war with Hamas, a war Hamas started by invading Israel on October 7, 2023, murdering 1,200 people and taking 251 hostage, most of whom were civilians. The genocide lie was initially propagated by left-wing anti-Israel activists and then adopted by right-wing Christian nationalists. Certainly, Palestinian non-combatants have tragically died in the war. Nevertheless, the falsity of calling it genocide is evident in that Israel had no intention to destroy, in whole or in part, the Palestinians in Gaza. In fact, Israel took extreme precautions in warning civilians to get out of harm's way while Hamas deliberately embedded among civilians to use them as human shields. Although it is heartrending that Palestinian non-combatants died, Israel was able to limit the ratio of civilian to combatant deaths to the lowest (2 to 1) in the history of modern urban warfare.[9] Civilian deaths are tragic, but they are an outcome of a just war, not genocide.

Another blood libel posted frequently is the allegation that Israel deliberately attacked a United States Navy vessel, the *USS Liberty*, during the Six-Day War of 1967. Although fringe right-wing Jew haters have long been made this accusation, the new Christian nationalists have now resurrected it. Although Israel did indeed attack the *USS Liberty*, it was a tragic case of mistaken identification. In fact, during the attack itself, as soon as the Israel Defense Forces realized its error, they ended their assault instantly and the Israeli navy launched search and rescue operations. According to Rich Lowery, editor of the conservative *National Review*, "The Israelis apologized immediately upon realizing their ghastly mistake and offered restitution." He concludes, "Both official Israeli and U.S. investigations determined that the attack was a friendly fire incident, but for Israel and the Jews in the current environment, the truth is no defense."[10]

Anti-Jewish Tropes

Comments on social media also contained classic anti-Jewish tropes accusing Jews of dual loyalties, control of media and movies and Israeli control of US policy. To say American Jews have dual loyalties or are "Israel firsters" fails to understand the US Jewish community's patriotism and love of country. In fact, since Jewish people were dispersed for millennia, Judaism teaches that they should support the government and leadership of their nation of residence.

Charges that the Jewish people control media and movies just repeats the longstanding resentment for Jewish success in multiple spheres. Alleging that Israel controls US policy through the "Jewish lobby" or AIPAC is nothing but a hateful slur. The American Israel Public Affairs Committee is a legal, registered United States lobbying group, representing more than six million pro-Israel US citizens, both Jewish and Gentile, from both the Democratic and Republican parties, as well as independent voters. This group is united by the legitimate desire for the US government to maintain strong ties with the state of Israel. At the same time, lobbies supporting the Arab cause and Arab countries, such as Qatar, give far more money to influence the US government and higher education. It is beyond inappropriate to single out the American Jewish community by launching slurs against it for legitimately advocating for its concerns, even as every other sub-group and industry does the same.

Other social media commenters complain that the United States provides some three billion dollars in foreign aid to Israel, as if these funds supply the basic needs for impoverished Israelis. Apparently, they are either unaware or willfully ignorant that this aid began only after the US pressured Israel to give up its own weapons manufacturing. Then, this subsidy was given for exclusive use to purchase US weaponry, thereby functioning as a US governmental subsidy to the American arms industry. The outcome of foreign aid has been beneficial to both governments through the joint development of weaponry such as the Iron Dome and Arrow anti-missile systems. The opposition to US aid to Israel is driven more by ignorance than fact.

CONCLUSION

What a shock it was to me as I observed so many comments on social media, clearly written by professing followers of Jesus, promoting hatred of the Jewish people. It reminded me of the behavior of the German church in the 1930s when the Nazi government arose. The German Christian Church then chose German nationalism and Jew hatred over kingdom righteousness and biblical values. Yet, the evil happening now seems worse to me in one distinctive way—the German church couldn't learn the lesson of the Holocaust. We can! We can see that hateful attitudes toward Jewish people can produce horrific crimes. As historian Ian Kershaw wrote, "The road to Auschwitz was built by hate, but paved with indifference."[11] Those who profess love for the Lord Jesus and still subscribe to Jew hatred, must repent of it. And those who don't embrace this hatred but are indifferent to it, must summon the courage to speak up and resist it (Prov. 24:10–12). We know where this can lead.

Acknowledgments

Writing a book is not a solitary act. As author Jeff Elkins says, writing "can't be done without a team of people around us." Therefore, I want to thank a number of people for their teamwork in producing this book.

I am grateful for Trillia Newbell, Acquisitions Director of Moody Publishers, who asked if I could produce this book on short notice. She thought I could, so I did. Also, thanks go to Drew Dyck, editor at Moody Publishers who oversaw all the details of this project. And I am so indebted to Pam Pugh, my long-time coworker at Moody, for her excellent work in editing this book. There are so many others at Moody Publishers that provided support including Janis Backing, Hope Francis, and Connor Sterchi. Thanks go to all of them.

Often people will think that biblical content, as found in this book, just flows out of the mind of an author. Nothing could be further from the truth. I have learned so much about what the Bible teaches about Israel and the Jewish people from Dr. Louis Goldberg, now with his Messiah Jesus, who was my teacher and Professor of Jewish Studies at Moody Bible Institute before me. Also, I'm grateful to my dear friend and mentor, Dr. Barry Leventhal, also with the Lord, who, when I was a graduate student, generously shared all his teaching notes and files with me. He also gave me a multitude of books, each time saying with a wink, that he happened to buy an extra one "by accident." Finally, many thanks go to my friend and teacher, Dr. Arnold Fruchtenbaum, who introduced me to a biblical theology of Israel, which he aptly named "Israelology."

Of course, my love and appreciation go to my wife, Eva, a brilliant teacher of God's Word and an excellent editor, who, before submission, read and edited every page, paragraph, sentence, and word. She made invaluable suggestions but always with grace, kindness, humor, and encouragement. The wisdom writer asked, "An excellent wife who can find?" (Prov. 31:10 ESV) and the obvious answer is, I did.

All these people, as well as others, certainly made this book better. Nevertheless, any faults or weaknesses in it remain my own.

Above all, I am grateful to the God and Father of Israel and His Son, Yeshua, the Messiah of Israel, who love the people of Israel with an everlasting love (Jer. 31:3). *Blessed are You, O Lord our God, King of the universe, who has granted us life, sustained us, and allowed us to reach this day. Amen.*

Notes

Chapter 1—Israel: Then and Now

1. *Hebrew*. This is an early term for the Israelite people, beginning with the patriarch Abraham (Gen. 14:13), perhaps derived from Abram descending from Eber (Gen. 10:21) or possibly from the Hebrew word *'ābar* ("to cross over"), since Abram crossed over the Euphrates River to come to the promised land (Josh. 24:2–3). The term was commonly used until discontinued just before David ascended to kingship (1 Sam. 29:3). Two exceptions for its later usage are in Jeremiah 34:9, 13, verses that allude back to earlier laws (Ex. 21:2–6). Significantly, in these later uses, Jeremiah equates the term "Hebrew" with "Jew" (Jer. 34:9). In the New Testament, a book written to ethnic Jewish followers of Jesus is called The Epistle to the Hebrews.

2. *Hebrew Language*. A second way the word "Hebrew" is commonly used today is of the Hebrew language, the language of the Old Testament Scriptures (except for a few chapters written in Aramaic). The Old Testament never uses this word of the language, but it does call the language "Judean" (2 Kings 18:26, 28) and "the language of Canaan" (Isa. 19:18). However, the New Testament does use the word Hebrew to designate the language of the Jewish people (John 5:2; 19:13, 17, 20; 20:16; Acts 21:40; 22:2; 26:14; Rev. 9:11; 16:16). With the dispersion of the Jewish people after first century AD following Rome's destruction of Jerusalem, Hebrew fell into disuse as a common language and became

a holy tongue reserved for prayer and religious study. With the Jewish enlightenment (the Haskalah) of the nineteenth century and the beginning of the Jewish return to the land of Israel (then called Palestine) in 1882, Hebrew was revived as a spoken language, especially under the efforts of Jewish linguist Eliezer Ben Yehuda. Today, it is the primary national language of the State of Israel (although Arabic is also an official language).

3. *Jacob*. The first use of the word Israel comes after the patriarch Jacob's wrestling match with God, when the Lord renamed Jacob, "Israel." The Lord said, "Your name shall no longer be Jacob, but Israel, for you have striven with God and with men and prevailed" (Gen. 32:28). The name means "God fights" or "He strives or persists with God."

4. *The Tribes of Israel*. Jacob had twelve sons, who later become the progenitors of twelve separate tribal groups of Israelites. Although the Scriptures repeatedly speak of twelve tribes, there is no normative listing of the twelve tribes in the Hebrew Bible. In fact, there are some twenty different lists in the Old Testament and only once is the same list repeated (Num. 2:3–31; 10:14–27). Nevertheless, all these lists are derived in some way from these twelve tribes.

5. *The People of Israel*. Initially, the Hebrew phrase *b'nay Yisrael* (sons of Israel) was reserved for Jacob's literal twelve sons. By the time of the Exodus, they were called Israel (Ex. 15:22). Ultimately, it became a phrase used for all the generations of the descendants of Jacob. Another expression, *Am Yisrael* (the people of Israel), was used for all the descendants of Abraham, Isaac, and Jacob, once they became a distinct ethnic nation (Josh. 8:33).

6. *The Land of Israel*. God had promised Abraham (Gen. 12:1, 7; 13:14–15; 15:18; 17:7–8), Isaac (Gen. 26:2–3), and Jacob (Gen. 28:13; 35:12) and all their descendants (1 Chron. 16:16–18; 2 Chron. 20:6–7)

the land of Canaan as their inheritance (Num. 34:1–29). Known as *Eretz Yisrael* or the Land of Israel, it had shifting boundaries at differing times but never achieved the expansive borders (from the River of Egypt to the Euphrates River) promised in Genesis 15:18. In the New Testament era, while under Roman domination, the land of Israel was called "the land of the Jews" (Acts 10:39).

7. *The Kingdom of Israel.* When the Lord named Saul as the first king of Israel (1 Sam. 9:1–27; 13:1), the people of Israel, in the land of Israel, became known as the Kingdom of Israel. Uniting the twelve tribes of Israel, the kingdom expanded under the reign of King David and then King Solomon. As such, it was the nation-state of the people of Israel.

8. *The Northern Kingdom of Israel.* In 930 BC, when King Solomon's son Rehoboam foolishly overburdened his subjects, the northern ten tribes of Israel rebelled and formed their own kingdom (1 Kings 12:1–24), known as the Kingdom of Israel. Initially led by King Jeroboam, the kingdom also was called Ephraim, and continued until it was conquered by the Assyrian King Sennacherib in 722 BC.

9. *The State of Israel.* Having been scattered and persecuted across the Diaspora for two millennia, at the end of the nineteenth century, some Jewish people, primarily from Eastern Europe, began to return to their ancient homeland, then known as Palestine. In 1896, Theodore Herzl began writing and organizing a Jewish return to the land of Israel, establishing what became known as the Zionist movement. After World War I, the League of Nations granted Great Britain a mandate to govern Palestine, requiring Britain to create a national homeland for the Jewish people in Palestine. After World War II, with Jewish people and local Arabs unable to live peaceably in Palestine, in 1947, the United Nations voted to partition the area of Palestine west of the Jordan River, into two separate states, one Jewish state and the other Arab. The Jewish community accepted the partition resolution but the

Arab nations did not. On May 14, 1948, with the end of the British Mandate, the National Council of the Jewish People in Palestine declared independence in the area of Palestine set apart for the Jewish state, adopting the name the State of Israel (*Medinat Yisrael*). Recognized immediately by the United States, the State of Israel was attacked by six neighboring Arab nations. With a victorious defense against invasion, the State of Israel was accepted shortly thereafter as a member state of the United Nations. Today, Israel is once again the nation-state of the Jewish people.

10. *The tribe of Judah*. The descendants of the patriarch Judah were promised ascendancy over the other tribes of Israel (Gen. 49:8–12) and occupied a central location in the Land of Israel. David, the second King of Israel, was from Judah, and his dynasty remained until the fall of the Judean Kingdom (586 BC).

11. *Southern Kingdom of Judah*. With the revolt of the ten northern tribes of Israel, the tribes of Judah and Benjamin united and formed the Kingdom of Judah (*Yehudah*), while remaining under the Davidic dynasty. In 586 BC, King Nebuchadnezzar of Babylon conquered the Kingdom of Judah, destroyed its capital Jerusalem and the Holy Temple Solomon had built, and exiled the people of Judah to Babylon (2 Kings 24:10–25:21).

12. *Jews*. After the exile to Babylon, both the exiled Judeans and those who remained behind in Judah began to be called Jews (*Yehudim*; Ezra 4:12, 23). While exiled in Babylon, those from the Northern Kingdom of Israel whom Assyria had previously taken captive joined with the Judean captives and also became known as Jews. By the New Testament era, the word "Jews" became synonymous for the covenant people Israel (Rom. 3:1; 9:4).

13. *Judea.* When the Roman Empire gained control of the land of Israel (63 BC), they divided it into districts, calling the southern district Judea. The northern district was called Galilee, and the central area was known as Samaria. In the New Testament, the whole area was called "the land of the Jews" (Acts 10:39). After the Second Jewish Revolt (AD 132–35), the Roman Emperor Hadrian renamed the land "Palestine," after the Philistines, the ancient enemies of Israel. He did this in order to attempt to eliminate the Jewish connection to Judea and suppress the Jewish identity of the land.

14. The actual meaning of the word "Zion" is unknown, but it has been suggested that it means "rock," "stronghold" ("Zion." *Encylopedia Judaica*. Edited by Cecil Roth, 1st Edition, [Jerusalem: Keter, 1972], 16:1030), or "place of defense," "fortress" (John Hartley, "Zion." *Theological Wordbook of the Old Testament*. Edited by R. Laird Harris, Gleason L. Archer, and Bruce K. Waltke [Chicago: Moody Publishers, 1980], 764). The meaning of the word has adapted over time. Initially, it referred to the Jebusite city David captured and then referred to the City of David, the original area of Jerusalem (2 Sam. 5:7).

15. *Mount Zion.* Once Solomon built the temple on Mount Moriah, the Temple Mount came to be called Mount Zion (Ps. 132:13–14). In the Byzantine era, between the 4th–7th centuries AD, early Christians misidentified the Western Hill of Jerusalem as Mount Zion, and the location is still known as Mount Zion today.

16. *City of Zion.* Although the Bible originally identified Mount Zion with the Temple Mount, later on it was used to refer to the city of Jerusalem (Isa. 2:3). Ultimately, "Zion" itself came to refer to the land of Israel (Isa. 51:11) and its people—"say to Zion, 'You are My people'" (Isa. 51:16).

17. *Zionism*. Zionism is perhaps one of the most misunderstood and misapplied terms in contemporary conversation. Some equate it with racism or bigotry, when in fact Zionism is merely the belief that Jewish people can rightfully have an autonomous state in their ancient homeland. It is nothing more than an ideology that calls for modern Jewish people to be free to exercise self-determination in the land of their origin. Sadly, the word "Zionist" has become a euphemism for Jewish people. As a result, it frequently provides cover for antisemitism (hatred of the Jewish people), so that some anti-Jewish bigots might say "No Zionists allowed" or "I'm anti-Zionist," but they actually mean "No Jewish people allowed," or "I'm admittedly anti-Jewish."

18. Thomas R. Schreiner, *Romans*, Baker Exegetical Commentary on the New Testament (Baker Books, 1998), 485.

19. C. E. B. Cranfield, *The Epistle to the Romans, Vol. II*, The International Critical Commentary, Editors J. A. Emerton and C. E. B. Cranfield (T & T Clark, 1979), 461.

20. Some have argued that Galatians 3:16 teaches that the true offspring (seed) of Israel is the Messiah Jesus, not the Jewish people. As such, only those related to the Lord Jesus by faith receive the benefit of the blessing for blessing/curse for curse principle. This is a misunderstanding of Galatians 3:16 that will be addressed in chapter 4 of this book.

21. The term "antisemitism" was coined in 1879 by Wilhelm Marr, a German political pamphleteer and founder of the Anti-Semitic League, a German political party. Marr intended to replace the German *Judenhass* (Jew Hatred) with a less vulgar, allegedly more scientific sounding word. The word has become a general term to denote all forms of hostility toward Jewish people throughout the centuries. I and many others spell this without a hyphen and use a lower case "s" because there is no such thing as a Semitic race or people. The word

refers exclusively to hatred of the Jewish people and not to any other linguistic or ethnic group. "Antisemitism" has morphed into a conspiracy theory that associates all the evils of the world as emanating from the Jewish people.

22. "ADL Report—Audit of U. S. Antisemitic Incidents 2024," April 22, 2025, Jewish Virtual Library, https://www.jewishvirtuallibrary.org/adl-report-audit-of-u-s-antisemitic-incidents-2024.
23. Press release: "ADL Launches Groundbreaking Jewish Policy Index to Assess State Policies to Combat Antisemitism, ADL, August 8, 2025, https://dc.adl.org/news/adl-launches-groundbreaking-jewish-policy-index-to-assess-state-policies-to-combat-antisemitism/.
24. Russell Contreras, "ADL: Antisemitic Incidents Hit Record Level in 2024," Axios, April 22, 2025, https://www.axios.com/2025/04/22/adl-survey-antisemitc-incidents-record-level-2024.
25. Thomas Friedman, "Campus Hypocrisy," *New York Times*, October 16, 2002.
26. Natan Sharansky, "3D Test of Anti-Semitism: Demonization, Double Standards, Delegitimization," *Jewish Political Studies Review* 16:3–4 (Fall 2004).
27. Taken from a photograph of the advertisement given to me personally by Dr. George Sweeting.

Chapter 2—Israel in the Center of History and Prophecy

1. Gail Lichtman, "Beating the Odds: Why Jews Win So Many Nobel Prizes," *Jerusalem Post*, May 11, 1997.
2. The personal promises God gave to Abraham included a great name, vast wealth, and abundant spiritual blessing for himself. The life of Abraham as recorded in Scripture confirms that these promises were

fulfilled. Significantly, the national promise of a future land called it an "everlasting possession." The universal promise would be that through Abraham the whole world would be blessed through Messiah (Gen.12:3).

3. Many Bible scholars call this "The Palestinian Covenant." However, since the use of the term "Palestine" is part of the political dispute today and never used in the Bible to describe the land of Israel, it is best to rename this promise from God the "Land Covenant."
4. The foretold descendant from "the stump of Jesse" and "the house of David" is announced in Isaiah 11:1,10; 16:5; Jeremiah 23:5; 30:9; 33:15–17; Ezekiel 34:23–24;37:24–28; Hosea 3:4–5; and Amos 9:11–15.
5. Paul Johnson, *A History of the Jews* (HarperPerennial, 1987), 3.
6. The Talmud, Nedarim 49b.
7. "Mark Twain: Concerning the Jews," *Harper's Magazine*, March 1898, https://archive.org/details/concerningthejew08mbp.

Chapter 3—Correcting Spiritual Identity Theft

1. Walter Gutbrod, in the authoritative *Theological Dictionary of the New Testament*, links Romans 2:28–29 to Romans 9:4–6 (to be discussed later in this chapter). He writes, "We are not told here that Gentile Christians are the true Israel." He maintains that the distinction here is similar to John 1:47, where Nathanael is called "a true Israelite indeed, in whom there is no deceit" not implying that others were no longer Israelites but that Nathanael exemplified a particular category of Israelites, those without deceit. Thus, he concludes that Rom. 2:28 does not imply that Paul is calling Gentiles the true Jews" but rather identifying a particular category of Jewish people, with both physical and spiritual circumcision. Walter Gutbrod, "Israel, k.t.l.," TDNT, III:387.

2. Michael G. Vanlaningham, "Romans," *The Moody Bible Commentary*, eds. Michael Rydelnik and Michael Vanlaningham (Moody Publishers, 2014), 1747.
3. Arnold G. Fruchtenbaum, *Israelology: The Missing Link in Systematic Theology* (Ariel Ministries, 1993), 684–90.
4. S. Lewis Johnson, "Paul and the Israel of God," in *Essays in Honor of J. Dwight Pentecost*, eds. Stanley D. Toussaint and Charles H. Dyer (Moody, 1986), 187.
5. Obviously, as discussed, some do hold that Romans 9:6–8 also refers to the church. But even many who affirm replacement theology interpret Romans 9:6 as referring to the Jewish remnant. It appears that Galatians 6:16 is the one passage that all supersessionists (i.e., those who hold that the church has replaced Israel) insist uses "Israel" to refer to the church.
6. David L. Turner, "Matthew 21:43 and the Future of Israel," *Bibliotheca Sacra* 159 (Jan–Mar 2002): 58–59.
7. "καινος" Frederick William Danker, Walter Bauer, William F. Arndt, and F. Wilbur Gingrich, *A Greek–English Lexicon of the New Testament and other Early Christian Literature*, 3rd ed. (University of Chicago Press, 2000), 496; J. Behm, "καινος," *Theological Dictionary of the New Testament* edited by Gerhard Kittel and Gerhard Friedrich, abridged by Geoffrey W. Bromiley (Eerdmans Publishing Company, 1985), 388.
8. John Stott, *The Message of Ephesians* (InterVarsity, 1979), 101–102.
9. There are a number of proposals regarding which Genesis blessing passage forms the basis of Paul's discussion in Galatians 3. The most helpful explanation is by C. John Collins, who identifies Genesis 22:17–18 as that passage in "Galatians 3:16: What Kind of Exegete Was Paul?," *TynBul* 54, no. 1 (2003): 75–86.

10. T. Desmond Alexander, "Further Observations on the Term 'Seed' in Genesis," Tyndale Bulletin 48.2 [1997]: 363–67.

Chapter 4—Why Christians Should Care About Israel and the Jewish People

1. A superficial reading would suppose that the Lord Jesus wept at the tomb of Lazarus out of grief for the death of a dear friend. In light of Jesus knowing that He was about to raise Lazarus from the dead, this is highly unlikely. In fact, this was exactly how the skeptical Jewish leaders misunderstood the tears of Jesus (11:36). A more careful reading would indicate that multiple Jewish people among the mourners had expressed a lack of faith in Jesus (Martha, 11:21; Mary, 11:32; the Jewish leaders, 11:37). These expressions of unbelief "deeply moved" (11:33) the Lord Jesus so that He wept (11:35). Therefore, John Hart concludes that Jesus' tears "were in response to the unbelief of the Jewish people" (John F. Hart, "John" *The Moody Bible Commentary*, eds. Michael Rydelnik and Michael Vanlaningham (Moody Publishers, 2014), 1640.

Afterword

1. Molly Minta and Michael Goldberg, "Suspect in Mississippi Synagogue Fire Laughed as He Confessed to His Dad, Authorities Say," *Mississippi Today*, January 12, 2026, https://mississippitoday.org/2026/01/12/mississippi-synagogue-fire-suspect-named/.
2. Charles Lee Feinberg, *A Commentary on Revelation: The Grand Finale* (BMH Books, 2020), 34.
3. This idea was popularized by a Marxist Jewish author, Arthur Koestler, whose intention was to end hatred of the Jews because of his contention that Jewish people were not genetically related to biblical Jewish

people but descended from the Khazars. See Arthur Koestler, *The Thirteenth Tribe* (Random House, 1976).

4. Michael Balter, "Tracing the Roots of Jewishness," *Science*, June 3, 2010, https://www.science.org/content/article/tracing-roots-jewishness.
5. Alexander Beider, "Ashkenazi Jews Are Not Khazars. Here's The Proof.," *Forward*, September 25, 2017, https://forward.com/opinion/382967/ashkenazi-jews-are-not-khazars-heres-the-proof/?attribution=author-article-listing-14-headline.
6. Prem Thakker, "White Supremacist Nick Fuentes Calls for 'Holy War' Against the Jews" *The New Republic*, July 17, 2023, https://newrepublic.com/post/174372/white-supremacist-nick-fuentes-calls-holy-war-jews?ref=maiseh-review.ghost.io; video, https://twitter.com/i/status/1680852059741106176 (accessed January 13, 2026).
7. As quoted in Heather Tomlinson, "Explained: Why Is Everyone Up in Arms About 'Christ Is King'"? *Premiere Christianity*, March 28, 2024, https://www.premierchristianity.com/news-analysis/explained-why-is-everyone-up-in-arms-about-christ-is-king/17450.article.
8. Bari Weiss, *How to Fight Anti-Semitism* (Crown Publishing, 2019).
9. Michael Rydelnik, "Israel Is Not Committing Genocide in Gaza," MichaelRydelnik.org, June 27, 2025, https://www.michaelrydelnik.org/blog/zez73bn2rlywxb2h2hdtq240qhy2th.
10. Rich Lowery, "No, the USS Liberty Attack Wasn't Israeli Treachery," *National Review*, December 23, 2025, https://www.nationalreview.com/2025/12/for-elements-of-the-anti-israel-right-everything-old-is-new-again/.
11. Ian Kershaw, *Popular Opinion and Political Dissent in the Third Reich, Bavaria 1933–1945* (Oxford University Press, 1983), 277.

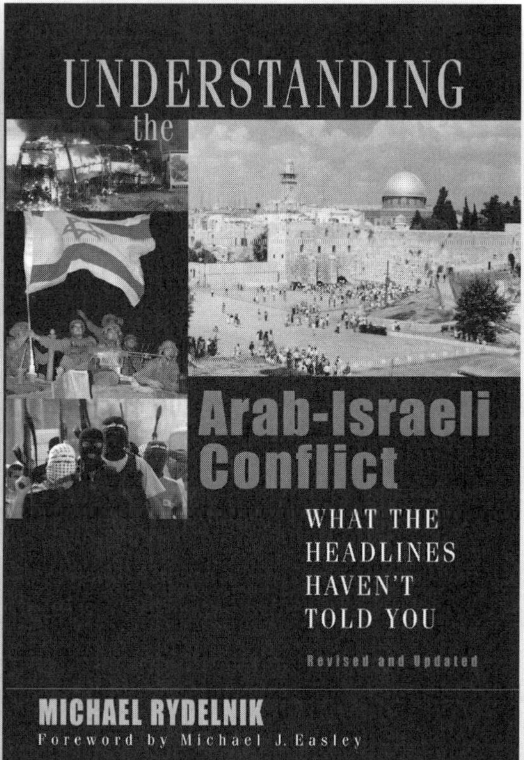

Now you can study the Bible with the faculty of the Moody Bible Institute!

Study the Bible with a team of 30 Moody Bible Institute professors. This in-depth, user-friendly, one-volume commentary will help you better understand and apply God's Word to all of life. Additional study materials include maps, charts, and bibliographies as well as a subject and Scripture index.

Also available as an eBook